MAKING TH
MOST OF

YOUR
SOCIAL
WORK
PLACEMENT

MAKING THE MOST OF
YOUR SOCIAL WORK PLACEMENT
PAULA BEESLEY

Los Angeles | London | New Delhi
Singapore | Washington DC | Melbourne

Los Angeles | London | New Delhi
Singapore | Washington DC | Melbourne

SAGE Publications Ltd
1 Oliver's Yard
55 City Road
London EC1Y 1SP

SAGE Publications Inc.
2455 Teller Road
Thousand Oaks, California 91320

SAGE Publications India Pvt Ltd
B 1/I 1 Mohan Cooperative Industrial Area
Mathura Road
New Delhi 110 044

SAGE Publications Asia-Pacific Pte Ltd
3 Church Street
#10-04 Samsung Hub
Singapore 049483

Editor: Catriona McMullen
Assistant editor: Ruth Lilly
Production editor: Martin Fox
Copyeditor: Solveig Gardner Servian
Proofreader: David Hemsley
Indexer: Judith Lavender
Marketing manager: Samantha Glorioso
Cover design: Wendy Scott
Typeset by: C&M Digitals (P) Ltd, Chennai, India
Printed in the UK

Library of Congress Control Number: 2019939052

British Library Cataloguing in Publication data

A catalogue record for this book is available from
the British Library

ISBN 978-1-5264-5895-7
ISBN 978-1-5264-5896-4 (pbk)

At SAGE we take sustainability seriously. Most of our products are printed in the UK using responsibly sourced
papers and boards. When we print overseas we ensure sustainable papers are used as measured by the PREPS
grading system. We undertake an annual audit to monitor our sustainability.

CONTENTS

ABOUT THE AUTHOR

Paula Beesley is a Senior Lecturer in Social Work at Leeds Beckett University, with interests in communication skill development and practice placements. She holds the Practice Teacher Award, and has been a practice teacher for 20 years both as a child protection social worker and as an independent off-site practice educator working with a wide range of placements and students. She is currently undertaking a PhD into communication in social work student supervision on placement.

PLACEMENT VOICES

The following people have provided contributions to the Placement Perspectives feature.

Fiona Adams is a childrens social worker, currently working as advanced practitioner in the Leeds Children's Health and Disabilities Teams. She is a practice educator and practice champion, and has supported a number of students. In her spare time she enjoys baking.

Siobhan Appleyard is a BA3 student at Leeds Beckett University. She is currently working on a child protection team for her final placement. Siobhan would like to continue to work with children and families as a Child Protection Social Worker. When she has gained experience as a social worker she aspires to work with adults as an approved mental health professional (AMHP).

Gail Barlow works independently as a practice educator (PE) and PE mentor. Having previously been employed as a mental health social worker she has worked as an off-site practice educator with students in voluntary as well as statutory settings. She now helps to deliver practice educator training. She lives with her partner and their two children.

Deklon Brown is a BA3 student at Leeds Beckett University, currently on his final placement within child protection for Leeds City Council. He plans to work within child protection while continuing his studies to complete a masters in psychological wellbeing. Eventually, he plans to specialise within Children and Adolescence Mental Health Services (CAMHS).

Loveworthy Chiguvo is a senior social worker within the adult social work team, with a background in the older people and learning disabilities work. She has specialism in practice education and is a practice champion, and has supported student social workers and practice educators through their progressions. Loveworthy is a best interest assessor (BIA). Away from work, she enjoys walking and spending time in the park.

Adele Clark is a final-year MA student at Leeds Beckett University, currently on placement in a very busy child protection locality team at Wakefield Council. She hopes to undertake an ASYE in a child protection team and during this time to discover areas of specialism that she may like to progress in. Adele's early thoughts of future career progression, based on her learning and experiences so far, include undertaking accredited training for working with parents with learning disabilities and progressing her qualification and knowledge to undertake AMPH training.

Hannah Cunningham is a BA3 student studying at Leeds Beckett University, currently on her final placement with children's social work services. She aspires to be a child protection social worker to build her knowledge and experience within this sector, and in the distant future hopes to become a team manager.

Megan Derrick is a BA3 student at Leeds Beckett University. At the time of writing, Megan is in her final statutory placement working within a children and families team. Post qualifying Megan looks to remain in a child protection position in order to complete her assessed and supported year in employment (ASYE) year.

Biraj Gurung, who was born in Nepal, is a newly qualified social worker, now working in his last placement, a busy mental health team in Leeds Adults Services.

Mary Harrison teaches on the social work programme at Leeds Beckett University. She is a placement tutor and freelance practice educator, working with students at all levels. She has experience and a particular interest in mental health social work.

Nicky Linacre is an independent reviewing officer with over twenty years social work experience, predominantly in the field of children and families. As an off-site practice educator she has worked with numerous universities in supporting many students in different placements, both voluntary and statutory. In her spare time Nicky enjoys reading cosy murder mysteries.

Hugo Macdonald-Hull is a BA3 student, currently on placement in a child protection team. Hugo is hoping to stay in child protection and develop his career in this field.

Stacey Mallinder is a BA3 student currently on her final placement in adult services. She aspires to work within the mental health sector before progressing to do the AMHP and BIA training.

Seonaid Matheson has used primarily mental health services for over twenty years. She started to engage with health and social work professionals whilst she was still a mental health social worker. She is a member of ABEL at Leeds Beckett University. She is now a freelance musician, playing violin and piano.

Myrtle Oke was born in the Caribbean and came to the UK in her teens. She is a retired nurse and midwife. She has had experiences with different professionals over the years, as a service user and a carer. She is a member of the Leeds Beckett University experienced lives involvement group (ABEL), and states that she gets involved because she believes that sharing her experiences will provide high-quality care and understanding of a social worker's perspective.

Julie Roome is a level 2 social worker working in a challenging adults' social work team in Wakefield. Julie is also a practice educator champion, ASYE assessor and a mentor. In her spare time, Julie enjoys walking with her Labradoodle and seeing her grandchildren.

Maryann Saviour is an ASYE social worker at North Yorkshire County Council. Working currently in Adults and Health, in the long term she aspires to become an AMHP. Her placements were in a voluntary children's team and a statutory adults team.

Freya Svendsen is a BA3 social work student currently on her final placement within a child protection team in Leeds. She is enjoying this placement and has settled into the team well. Freya plans to do her ASYE within a Leeds Local Authority Child Protection team.

Sarah Taylor has been employed as a social worker by Leeds City Council for the last ten years. For the last six of these years she has been an advanced practitioner and practice educator. She is passionate about sharing her knowledge and experience with social work students and social workers on their ASYE. Sarah currently plays an active role in the Leeds and Wakefield Teaching Partnership.

Sophie Turnbull is a newly qualified social worker working within a children's health and disability team in Leeds. Her interest is in working with parents who have a disability.

ACKNOWLEDGEMENTS

I would like to thank my amazing family who support my passion for writing, Adrian, Lily and James.

I would also like to thank every social work student that I have supported as a practice educator, tutor and senior lecturer. Without your triumphs, challenges and reflections where we explore issues together, I would not understand social work placements in the same way. Thank you to every practice educator who provides a practice learning opportunity to a social work student, you are the bedrock of the future of social work.

Paula

INTRODUCTION

Many social work students are excited by the prospect of their placement, often citing that this is the opportunity 'to do' social work. This book will support you, the student, to develop an understanding that your placement is a learning opportunity which is so much more than *doing*: it should be underpinned by knowledge, skill and value development that will enable you to offer excellent interventions to service users and maximise your potential to develop into an effective and capable social worker.

Gill and Medd (2015: 12–14) suggest that students should make 'each day relevant ... (and) ... meaningful'. This is great advice both in university and on placement. Embrace learning from every day and every learning opportunity. This is *your* learning experience: use it. This book will help you to identify your individual learning needs, so that you can ensure that you consolidate your strengths whilst building your skills in other areas with the support of your practice educator. The core message of this book is that you should see placement as a wonderful experience to develop who you are on a personal and professional level, and to embrace every learning opportunity with proactive enthusiasm. Your social work placement is the first opportunity for you to apply your learning at university to your practice. By developing an inquisitive and proactive approach to enhancing your practice on placement, that enthusiasm to learn should be embedded for your whole career.

Social work criteria have developed along a number of avenues, and different social work courses will use these in different ways. Knowledge and Skills Statements (KSS) provide guidance for qualified childrens social workers (DfE, 2018) and adults social workers (DoH, 2015), and the Standards of Proficiency for Social Workers in England (SOPs) (HCPC, 2017b) are the criterion for social work registration. Both, along with the Professional Capability Framework (PCF) (BASW, 2018), discussed in more detail below and shown in Figure 0.1, are often applied within social work education. These are guides that provides guidance and expectation of the development of specific relevant skills and knowledge for that area of practice, which are very useful in your development. E-links to each of these are provided at the end of the Introduction as further reading.

The PCF (BASW, 2018) is the main criterion used within this book. It is the English framework that sets out the requirements for social workers' skills at different stages of their career, including social work students' assessment. It provides nine domains to meet, and details the level that you are required to meet at different stages within your career. Consequently, it is a developmental framework which advocates that social work professionals should never become complacent in thinking that they have learnt everything possible, and recommends continual reflection and development of new skills throughout their career. As such, see your social work placement as the start of a long, but enjoyable, career where learning should be central to your core values.

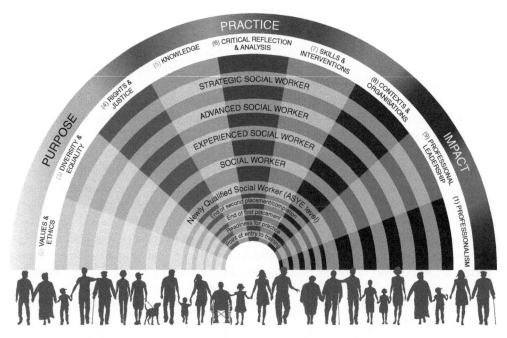

Figure 0.1 The PCF fan (BASW, 2018). Reproduced with kind permission of BASW.

The further positive of the PCF (BASW, 2018) is that it demands that you look at your skill development holistically. You cannot undertake a good-quality intervention without understanding and reflecting upon the professional expectations on you, your own value base, the societal and individual oppression a service user may have experienced, the theory you will have used, and the organisational procedure and legislative basis of the work. Your interventions cannot be seen in isolation; a good social work student is able to reflect upon their own practice whilst understanding with empathy the actions of others.

■■■■ PLACEMENT PERSPECTIVE 0.1 ■■■■

Practice educator's expectation of a social work student on placement

When I was asked to consider what I expect from a social work student on placement, my overriding response was *professionalism*. I have worked with such a wide range of students with differing personal styles and strengths but professionalism covers all the bases and is essentially what gets a student through their placement successfully. Good communication is obviously vital, with both your practice educator and service users. However, above all I need to see that you, the student, want to learn, that you are organised, self-motivated and actively engaging in the opportunities available. Here is what I need to see you demonstrating:

- Prepare for your pre-placement meeting and put real thought into what your learning needs are for this placement. Establish what you really want to get out of this experience.
- Manage your time and be prepared for hard work over the course of the placement. Plan to make the best use of your study time as well as setting time aside at home to make sure you complete all the academic and placement tasks within agreed timeframes. It is understood that whilst on placement you are essentially working and studying at the same time.
- Come prepared for supervision, this is your time. Have an agenda and bring examples of your experiences and practice. Do your 'homework', complete any reading or research tasks and feed this knowledge back into future discussions.
- Be committed to the reflective process, both verbally and in writing. Be genuinely open to exploring your thoughts and feelings about the work. Ban the words 'I don't know' and be willing to say the wrong thing rather than

nothing at all. This can be a challenge when seeking support from the same person who is assessing your placement, but you can only get out as much as you are prepared to put in.

- Make reference to your knowledge and learning in written reflections when weighing up relevant issues. It might seem obvious to you, but you need to break down your thought processes, your judgements and your decision making.
- Maintain a clear sense of purpose and awareness of your role with service users. Why are you there, what is your remit and who is your client?
- Remain curious! Ask questions. Stay enthusiastic and seek out opportunities to undertake tasks and work with other professionals and agencies to broaden your understanding and perspective.
- Respond to the advice and experience of others whilst being able to defend your views and justify your opinions.
- Finally, speak up if you are struggling or finding situations difficult and accept the support available. The practice educator is much more likely to be sympathetic and able to negotiate solutions if you are honest and open from the start.

The nature of your working relationship with the practice educator can really influence your experience of the placement and it is worth making your own list of what you expect from them. This can then be shared at the start of your placement to develop a supervision agreement.

Gail Barlow, Off-site Practice Educator

COLLABORATIVE PRACTICE EDUCATION

Throughout this book, you will find a focus on the support that you can expect from your practice educator, and an emphasis on what you need to contribute to maximise your learning from your placement. However, underpinning both of those elements is the benefit of collaborative learning, where you combine both those elements and responsibilities to capitalise on the skills and knowledge that you each have. If you perceive that you are both experts, the practice educator in social work skills and you, the social work student, in yourself, your learning needs and learning style, then by combining both sets of knowledge and expertise you can enhance your ability to engage with the learning process.

Sennett (2008) recommends, when developing a new skill, a collaborative approach between student and mentor which utilises the mentor's breadth of knowledge and experience to enhance the student's learning, motivate their progression, and respects the student's individualised skill development. He argues that as the student becomes increasingly confident and competent, they should be facilitated to question and challenge the mentor, with the mentor exploring the student's response constructively. Within your social work placement, you will be expected to be participant in reflective discussion in supervision that enables you to identify your strengths and areas for development with the collaborative support of your practice educator. These will enhance your ability to critically analyse an intervention and enhance your understanding of the multiple factors that influence service provision. The role of the practice educator in collaborative practice education is to stimulate you to identify your own learning needs, and support you to address them yourself. Collaborative practice education enables the social work students to be empowered, respected and participant in their own development.

Types of placement opportunities

> Practice placements settings should be with a wide range of user groups including where there are integrated care pathways that draw on wider community services and resources.
> (Croisdale-Appleby, 2014: 86)

Social work comes in a wide variety of forms, and social work courses reflect that breadth of opportunity. If you are on a university route, you will be offered a minimum of two placements that expand your experience, prepare you to work within a statutory social work setting and meet your identified learning needs. Your two placements should be *different*, often interpreted as one childrens service and one adults service placement, but sometimes as different services within either area. Essentially it should enable you to learn different skills and understand different service provision. Your university will have an agreed placement procedure, and that does vary across the country. Additionally, there are new social work qualification routes which vary significantly from this model, including apprenticeships and paid fast-track MA routes, which may have longer in a work-based location, not necessarily called placement. Some social work students will be enabled to undertake a first placement in their own work place, and the challenge for them is to ensure that they are afforded new experiences to ensure that the placement is still developmental and that they are supported to see the placement through a social work reflective lens. This book does not aim to cover every placement type, but works within some general models of placement; the philosophy of enthusiastic learning remains the same wherever you are placed.

Your practice educator is required to be a qualified social worker and a qualified or qualifying practice educator (BASW, 2013). You should receive weekly supervision, both formal and informal supervision, and the team within which you are placed will be an excellent source of information and support too. Some voluntary placements will have an unqualified practice supervisor, who facilitates your day-to-day learning (the management element), with an off-site practice educator (OSPE) to provide the education, assessment, and assessment elements of the ESMA model of supervision (Doel, 2010) as discussed in Chapter 3 in regular supervision sessions.

Your first placement may be in a voluntary agency, a statutory social care setting or a statutory fieldwork team with less complex practice learning opportunities allocated to you. The aim of the placement is for you to develop your understanding of a service user group, your communication and organisational skills, and undertake practice learning opportunities with support. The PCF (BASW, 2018: 22–28) outlines how a student should be able to meet each domain 'with guidance'. The first placement enables you to explore your strengths and identify your learning needs; it is a time to reflect on your own and others' practice to begin to develop the skills required to become a social worker.

In comparison, your second placement requires you to develop your social work skills further and be able to begin to work more independently. Most social work courses will allocate a statutory fieldwork placement for your second placement. The work should be more complex, and you should be able to undertake more complex practice learning opportunities. The PCF (BASW, 2018: 29–36) outlines how a student should be able to 'demonstrate' and 'take responsibility for' each domain. The second placement enables you to develop your confidence in decision making, take the lead in interventions and demonstrate professionalism whilst consolidating your ability to reflect on your skill development.

Irrespective of the placement, if you engage with the learning opportunities and maximise your learning, you will not just have passed placement, you will also have developed your skills, knowledge and values to enable you to become a capable social worker.

LEARNING FEATURES

Throughout the book, the writing is supplemented with a range of core learning features:

Placement perspectives

At the start and the end of each chapter, there is a section providing the perspectives of involved others on the chapter's themes. This includes the views of students, NQSWs, practice educators, a tutor and a service user, who all have different but very valuable perspectives that should be considered as you move through the book (see Placement Voices at the beginning of the book).

Reflective tasks

Throughout the book you will be asked to reflect upon your own perspective, values, skills and thoughts on the chapter's themes to enable you to apply the theory to your own practice.

Potential placement pitfalls and opportunities

Each chapter provides examples of how different students approached the same dilemma and highlights the potential outcomes dependent on the responses. When reading these learning features you are encouraged to reflect upon their relevance to your practice, and how you can maximise your own learning outcomes.

Chapter checklist

Each chapter concludes with a checklist of key points from the chapter to support your development.

Further reading

Finally you are provided with relevant further reading to enable further understanding of topics from the chapter.

CHAPTER SUMMARIES

This book works with you from start of placement, where you will be asked to understand own learning needs and university procedures, through the placement itself, where you will be asked to reflect on your relationship with the practice educator and service users and your skill development, and finishes with discussion on the academic requirements that support your placement development, including reflection, evidence gathering and assignment writing.

Chapter 1 will explore you, the social work student, as an individual learner. It will ask you to consider your own learning style, in order to support you to understand how to best meet your learning needs. There will be a discussion about motivation to learn, and the need, as an adult learner, to be proactive in using your learning opportunities. It will introduce the concept of developing your emotional intelligence by reflection on your own learning needs, including both strengths that you can consolidate and areas for development, in addition to reflection on the importance of strong emotional resilience, so that you can maximise your learning on placement.

Chapter 2 will support the social work student to understand how to successfully engage with the university processes that frame the placement and assess the student. It will work through the placement process and address how to successfully complete the placement application form, informal meeting, placement learning agreement meeting, direct observation, interim and final report and meeting. The remit here is to maximise learning through each procedure.

Chapter 3 will reflect on how to establish and develop a positive and collaborative working relationship when the practice educator is both your mentor and assessor, and will contemplate professional boundaries. It will consider different aspects of supervision and how to use supervision to support your development.

Chapter 4 will ask the student social worker to reflect on the importance of the service user (and carer) within their social work placement. It will focus on keeping the service user central to their learning and practice development. It will ask the student social worker to consider the impact of self on the service user, and will conclude with an exploration of gathering service user feedback.

Chapter 5 will provide discussion on the need for the social work student to develop understanding of a breadth of skills, including professionalism, the ability to apply theory to practice and the skill of understanding their own and other's values, discussing often complex ethical dilemmas. The student will be asked to reflect throughout on their own skill development and the holistic nature of being a social worker.

Chapter 6 will concentrate on guidance and support on enhancing your ability to reflect. Consideration will be given as to why and how to undertake critically reflective writing, including exploration of different reflection models. The chapter will also explore verbal reflection in supervision and informal discussion, and personal ongoing reflection. As with previous chapters, there will be a discussion on collaborative learning with your practice educator.

Chapter 7 will reflect on how to respond positively when your practice educator provides you with constructive feedback. This may be that you need to address developmental areas to consolidate and enhance your practice, or it may be that the progress on placement is not going as planned. It will consider the expectations on a social work student, and what 'good enough' practice is. It will offer advice throughout to the student, with a clear focus on the need to reflect on their own practice to enhance their holistic skills and capability, whilst using collaborative learning with the practice educator. The philosophy is to aid the reader to identify ways to avoid the placement situation deteriorating further, but will also consider the ultimate outcome of a failed placement.

Chapter 8 will explore the expectations of compiling an evidence portfolio. It will offer advice on how to do this, including tips, strategies and advice. The chapter will provide examples of how to maximise evidence matching so that your evidence folder represents the breadth of work you have undertaken on placement and represents you well. By examining your learning from work undertaken, you are likely to enhance your development as you connect individual activity into holistic learning and are afforded the opportunity to reflect on your development from it.

Chapter 9 will provide generic advice on placement assignment writing, and acknowledge variety across university placement assignments. It will look at the core themes that asks the student to write an assignment based on the ability to match an intervention to specified criteria; an assignment that asks the student to provide a case study that analyses theories and skills used; and an assignment that demands reflection on learning from placement. The style of assignment will vary, but the common theme will be an expectation for a more reflective style of writing. It will consider how to identify future learning needs and include them in assignment.

━━━━━━━━━━━━━━━━━━━ PLACEMENT PERSPECTIVE 0.2 ━━━━━━━━━

Social work student's perspective on placement learning opportunities

I believe that my time on placement gave me the ability to bridge the work I had learnt in a university setting to actual real-life scenarios. Although I had a foundation of knowledge built from university of what to expect and how to adapt to life on placement, I found myself worrying about how everything linked. The open and honest relationship I developed with my practice educator challenged me to think of the scenario from a different perspective, allowing my reflective work to develop. I quickly realised that it all moulds together and reflecting on my values and the social work theories with my practice enabled me to delve further and develop my understanding. I used my practice educator to develop build my confidence and enhance the work I undertook.

I strongly believe that you only get out what you put in: seizing every opportunity to develop my practice and reflect on my learning helped me to apply what I had learnt academically into real practice and develop my learning further.

Megan Derrick, BA Social Work Student

CONCLUSION

This book could be seen to have a superficial goal to support you to pass your placement, but instead demands of the reader a more reflective approach to placement with the beneficial aim to support you to develop your personal and professional values, skills and knowledge to enable you to optimise your learning and make the most of your social work placement.

━━━━━━━━━━━━━━━ **Further reading** ━━━━━━━━━━━━━━━

Department of Health (DoH) (2015) *Knowledge and Skills Statement for Social Workers in Adult Services*. Available at: www.gov.uk/government/consultations/adult-social-work-knowledge-and-skills (accessed 16 April 2019).

Department for Education (DfE) (2018) *Post-qualifying Standard: Knowledge and Skills Statement for Child and Family Practitioners*. London: HMSO. Available at: www.gov.uk/government/publications/knowledge-and-skills-statements-for-child-and-family-social-work (accessed 16 April 2019).

British Association of Social Workers (BASW) (2018) *Professional Capability Framework*. Available at: www.basw.co.uk/professional-development/professional-capabilities-framework-pcf (accessed 16 April 2019).

Health and Care Professions Council (HCPC) (2017) *Standards on Proficiency: Social Workers in England*. London: HCPC. Available at: www.hcpc-uk.org/standards/standards-of-proficiency/ (accessed 16 April 2019).

1

GETTING TO KNOW YOURSELF AS A LEARNER

Chapter 1 will explore you, the social work student, as an individual learner. It will ask you to consider your own learning style in order to support you to understand how to best meet your learning needs. There will be a discussion about motivation to learn, and the need, as an adult learner, to be proactive in utilising your learning opportunities. It will introduce the concept of developing your emotional intelligence by reflection on your own learning needs, including both the strengths that you can consolidate and areas for development, in addition to reflection on the importance of strong emotional resilience, so that you can maximise your learning on placement.

===== **PLACEMENT PERSPECTIVE 1.1** =====

Practice educator's perspective on an emotionally intelligent social work student

As a practice educator I am not looking for all students to behave or act the same. There is diversity in all areas of humanity within our families, friendship groups, university friends and of course within service user groups. As a practice educator I expect all students to come from different backgrounds, bring different experiences to placement and also to have different learning styles. However, there are some characteristics I look for in all students beginning placement and that provide a strong indicator that a placement will be successful.

The first of these is that a student is prepared for the placement opportunity offered. It is evident at an initial placement meeting when a student demonstrates enthusiasm for the learning opportunity. It is important for a student to be able to demonstrate an awareness of their own expectations and learning needs for the placement. A good student will have read through the PCF before the placement starts, and will have started to think how these could be met during the placement. This is important because it

(Continued)

demonstrates to the practice educator that they are already invested in their learning.

I am always impressed to see a student who has begun to consider their own personal values and experiences in relation to the service user group. This is very important because a student's own life experiences could have a significant impact on their ability to engage in the practice learning opportunity. For example, a care leaver placed in a statutory social work team will need to consider how their own lived experiences might impact on the placement both positively and negatively.

It is also important that a student has begun to consider their own existing knowledge and experience that they will be bringing to the placement. As a practice educator I value the experience students bring to placement. However, this also includes considering any gaps in the student's knowledge and experience; this will help the practice educator identify training and learning opportunities within the placement to address these.

While all this preparation is very important, the most important thing I am looking for in a student is a willingness to learn and an ability to be proactive in engaging in the practice learning opportunity.

Sarah Taylor, Practice Educator

Fenge et al. (2014) argue that placements are influenced by your existing skills and knowledge, your learning needs and expectations, and your preferred learning style. Each of these areas will be considered as the chapter progresses. Future chapters will discuss other influences on your placement success, including your relationship with your practice educator. Doel (2018) reminds us that whilst every student has a different starting point, they all have to get over the final line to successfully complete placement. He believes that a strong placement and skilled practice educator supports the student to develop uniquely to achieve this.

EXPLORING YOUR MOTIVATION

Social work is a challenging (and rewarding) career that will demand of you a competent level of communication skills, decision making skills, analytical skills and interprofessional working skills that will enable you to support and safeguard the most vulnerable people in our society. The development of competency in such skills is critical to ensure quality service provision, so the development and assessment of your skills is essential to safeguard the future integrity of the profession, as discussed in Chapter 5.

I recommend that, before you start placement, you ask yourself why you are going on a social work placement. You will all have different and individualised motivations for becoming a social worker and doing your chosen route. Answer honestly. If you recognise that it is a means to an end, then it is possible that you will not see the benefit of it as a learning opportunity. If you are beginning to review if social work is the correct career for you, seek help from a tutor to discuss this. A positive choice, no matter the outcome, is always positive. It is the reflection on the outcome that merits praise as it demonstrates emotional intelligence.

How will you sustain your enthusiasm and commitment when you are on placement and you also have educational and personal commitments?

By understanding your motivation to undertake this often stressful assessment period, you are beginning to formulate a *positive mental attitude*, which is frequently associated with a positive outcome.

> More than any other single factor, your mindset will determine the success of your placement; and success is not just about pass or fail but about how enjoyable it is and how much it really stretches you as a person and a professional. (Doel, 2010: 54)

Additionally, think about why you will complete placement tasks. If you write the placement assignment to get an academic grade or attend a meeting to tick the box of completing inter-professional working, you will see it strategically. If you see these tasks as a way to enhance your knowledge and skills, you will be developing your understanding of the complexities of being a social worker, which will in turn enhance your ability to be a social worker. I would strongly recommend that you see all learning opportunities as just that: opportunities to learn. Occasionally they may not present immediate relevance for your career development, however, they will always be beneficial to your holistic social work education. Furthermore, your practice educator will be delighted with your commitment and enthusiasm and engage in your learning.

POTENTIAL PLACEMENT *PITFALL* Becky wanted a placement working with adults experiencing mental health problems, but was placed in a placement working with adults with learning difficulties. She immediately complained to her peers and told the placement in the informal pre-placement meeting that she was not interested in their placement. The practice educator tried to engage Becky and gave her different experiences within the induction period. However, the lack of interest she displayed disengaged the team and the practice educator's enthusiasm waned.

POTENTIAL PLACEMENT *OPPORTUNITY* Halima wanted a placement working with adults experiencing mental health problems, but was placed in a placement working with adults with learning difficulties. She made an appointment to speak to her tutor, who helped her recognise the transferability of skills between different service user groups, and the breadth of learning opportunities she would have. Halima volunteered to participate in a capacity assessment to understand the process, and throughout placement explored and reflected on how mental health issues impacted on service users with a learning difficulty. The practice educator never knew of Halima's dilemma, and commented in the final report on her commitment and enthusiasm.

SOCIAL WORK STUDENT CHARACTERISTICS

As a student studying social work, there are certain core characteristics that you will be required to develop and demonstrate. Although transferred to Social Work England (SWE) in 2019, much of the Health and Care Professions Council (HCPC) documentation remains relevant to good social work practice. The key attributes that the HCPC (2017a) highlights as expectations of you as a social work student are shown below. Reflect for a moment on each and consider how you will meet each one whilst on placement, and identify if there are any areas that you feel might be more difficult for you.

Guidance on Conduct and Ethics for Students, HCPC (2017a)

1 Promote and protect the interests of service users and carers
2 Communicate appropriately and effectively
3 Work within the limits of your knowledge and skills
4 Delegate appropriately
5 Respect confidentiality
6 Manage risk
7 Report concerns about safety
8 Be open when things go wrong
9 Be honest and trustworthy
10 Keep records of your work with service users and carers

Your practice educator will not be looking for perfection in these areas, but for a social work student who strives towards it and demonstrates the best practice that you can at that time. It is commitment to learn that engages the practice educator, and an eagerness to develop that passes the placement. This book takes this guidance and considers that as a social worker you will be required to develop the skills to demonstrate the ability to be able to communicate effectively, including assertively when required; to intervene to maximise outcomes; to reflect on work undertaken; to be able to apply theory to practice; to be professional; and to be able to recognise your values and how they impact on your service provision; all with an understanding of the social policy, legislative and societal positions we hold. Other expectations include demonstrating accountability through seeking support and advice when appropriate whilst being able to work independently, showing initiative and accountability as both an individual worker and team player. But most of all, you must show the ability to adapt and develop throughout your career.

Knowles (1973) discussed that adults learn in a different way from children and proposed adult learning theory, or andragogy. He argued that adult learners are self-motivated, ready and orientated to learn, and that is most definitely an attitude that your practice educator will expect and assess. You can only benefit from preparing yourself in the best possible way to maximise your learning whilst on placement, taking responsibility for accessing the learning opportunities provided, and being proactive in all aspects of placement. Knowles argued that adult learners in new learning situations call on their existing knowledge and skills to approach the new task.

When approaching placement, do not be afraid that you know nothing but look at what you *do know* how to do, and use those skills as a foundation on which to build. For example, we all communicate socially, so use those skills in an increasingly refined way to communicate with service users and professionals. You have organised yourself in university and life to achieve arriving at this point, so use those organisational skills whenever you are given a practice learning opportunities to manage. Have confidence in the skills you have whilst acknowledging the areas you will need to enhance further.

A key theme as you develop as a social work student is to reflect on your practice. An understanding of your strengths to enable you to draw upon them in challenging situations is central to developing your skills, whilst understanding of your areas for development enables you to identify where to focus. Chapter 6 discusses different ways to reflect, and should be read in conjunction with this chapter.

UNDERSTANDING YOUR INDIVIDUAL LEARNING NEEDS

Clearly, there is a minimum level of skill and knowledge that you need to demonstrate as you progress through your course. In England the PCF (BASW, 2018) is the measure by which social work students on placement are assessed. At the core of any social work assessment framework is the development of intervention skills, theoretical knowledge, understanding of values and diversity, and an ability to reflect on practice.

Nevertheless, where you begin, and how far you develop, is a more individualised approach. You have individual learning needs, specific strengths and areas for development, and a distinct learning style, and we all develop at different speeds and in different ways. You should never see yourself as being on a social work qualification conveyor belt because every social worker student should be on their own learning trajectory. Some of you will have come straight from school with limited volunteering experience, others will have clear and relevant experience after a career in social care agencies or a caring role, or you may have had non-related experience in engineering or business. There will be students from all social classes and ethnicity, British and international. All will bring relevant and interesting stories and experiences, but each of you is unique. Please do not compare your peers' adventures on placement on social media because theirs will always sound more exciting than yours, but instead reflect upon your learning needs because it is only by doing so that you will be able to understand, embrace and address them. In Chapter 3 we discuss Vygotsky's (1978) zone of peripheral development, where the practice educator should support you to develop from where you are now to fulfil your potential. Within your placement you will be allocated work that meets your current ability and your current learning needs.

Throughout this book you will be asked to reflect on your learning needs – these are your areas for development, and what you do well, your strengths. If one works from a strengths perspective, you, your university and your placement should recognise and build on your strengths to enable you to have stable foundations on which to identify and address your areas for development.

Reflective Task 1.2

Complete Table 1.1 to start you thinking about one strength and one area for development for each of the skills.

Table 1.1　Key attributes of a social work student

Skill	Strength	Area for development
Professionalism, i.e. time management skills, stress management		
Understanding of your values		
Ability to apply theory to practice		
Intervention and communication skills		

Please do not feel restricted to one if you think of several, but do ensure that you have equal numbers of strengths and areas for development. This is not meant to be a celebration of your skills or a bombardment of your failures, but rather a starting point to help you think about the level of the key social work student skills that you already possess and direct you to start your skill development pre-placement to aid your in-placement progress. It should also assist you in identifying your placement learning needs, which are required when completing your placement application form and presentation in informal and formal pre-placement meetings, where you should create a personalised reflection of your learning needs and skills that engages your practice educator as they see your potential, as discussed in Chapter 2.

Do not see placement learning in isolation, but consider available educational support as an invaluable resource that can prepare you for placement and support you whilst on placement. For example, many universities run support sessions on how to enhance time management skills, a key social work skill that can influence the outcome of your placement. If you know that you are not the most organised of students, by attending such a support session, developing recommended coping strategies, and addressing an assessed area of development of your organisational skills before you go on placement, your ability to engage with the placement learning will be enhanced. Cabiati and Folgheraiter (2019) argue that if you undertake such a task to enhance your own understanding of yourself and develop your skills, you will build empathy for service users and strengthen your social work skills further too.

Reflective Task 1.3

Without dismissing your strengths, do you have an area of development that frequently is identified by you, your peers, colleagues, tutor or supervisor?

How will you access support before your placement begins?

What coping strategy techniques can you identify that will enhance this area whilst on placement?

....

This is not to say that by developing a coping strategy that you are becoming a strategic learner, as these are two quite different things. A coping strategy helps you to learn, whereas a strategic learner undertakes a task from a way that they know will demonstrate competence to the assessor, in other words to tick a box with no intent to enhance longer-term practice. I would take a moment to warn those of you who are attracted to the notion that social work students on placement who are strategic learners are never found out, as maintaining a façade for a prolonged period of assessment is impossible.

By comparison, a coping strategy begins as an unfamiliar way to support you work more efficiently and effectively in the context of an area of development, which then goes on to become an internalised way of working that enhances your everyday practice as it becomes your normal behaviour. Discuss with your practice educator the need to achieve small tasks successfully if you are feeling overwhelmed. This will enable you to build your self-confidence and support you to tackle the more substantial learning opportunities.

UNDERSTANDING YOUR INDIVIDUAL LEARNING STYLE

To help you start to think about developing new or existing social work skills, it will help if you understand your best way to learn. If you are able to talk to your practice educator about your favoured way to learn, they will be able to adjust your induction and their teaching, so that you can optimise your learning and therefore enhance your outcomes.

There are a number of learning styles theories, but the two most favoured in social work are Honey and Mumford (1986) and VARK (Fleming and Mills, 1992). Honey and Mumford (1986) argue that there are four styles of learner: activist, reflector, theorist and pragmatist. They provide a questionnaire that facilitates the identification of your favoured learning style. It should be noted that that does not mean that you should learn using only the one style, as this will restrict your development. Instead, it gives a framework for you to understand your favoured learning style, so that you can focus on it when you are struggling. The most advantageous way of learning would be considered to be the use of all the styles: prepare in advance as a theorist, be a pragmatic activist who is open to trying new activities and learning as you go, whilst being able to reflect on the learning afterwards. If you see similarities with Kolb's (1984) reflective cycle, well done: Honey and Mumford based their learning styles on it.

Another useful way for you to understand the best way for you to learn is VARK (Fleming and Mills, 1992), which also gives different preferred learning styles: visual, aural, read/write and kinesthetic. When translated into social work placement learning, this is evidenced by whether you learn best by observing your practice educator's practice (visual), discussing and reflecting in informal and formal supervision (aural), reading in preparation/taking notes to review about instruction (read/write) or practical activities (kinesthetic). As with Honey and Mumford's learning styles, VARK should be used as a guide to understand the best way to learn for you whilst using all three styles to maximise your growth.

....

POTENTIAL PLACEMENT *PITFALL* Harriet was finding it difficult to understand the referral system at her placement. She knew that she needed to gather information and record her work to reflect her decision making in regard to whether the service user's needs met the service provision criteria, but could not understand how to use the IT system. She had asked her practice educator, who had calmly the second time but with less patience the fourth time explained the process to her. Concerns were raised about her ability to develop within the agency's framework.

POTENTIAL PLACEMENT *OPPORTUNITY* Lauren was finding it difficult to understand the referral system at her placement. In order to understand the process, she first listened to her practice educator's explanation of the importance of the system so that she understood the context and process of referrals within the wider service provision context. But Lauren knew that she was a visual learner, so she then asked to observe referrals from a variety of colleagues so that she could see how different people approached the task. She reflected on how she would approach the task and made notes on the process of taking and recording a referral, and the other information that she needed to gather to enable her to make a decision in regard to whether the service user's needs met the service provision criteria. Finally, she started to use the system herself. Whilst she initially missed a step, she was able to refer to her notes and discuss with her practice educator and soon became confident and competent with the referral system.

....

If you approach a new task initially in your favoured way to develop your confidence, that should enable you to use other styles that facilitate a depth of learning and understanding so that you do not negate or ignore valuable teaching. This example is not to say that you should learn in this exact way, but that you should understand yourself so that you can help your practice educator to support your development most effectively. It also shows the collaborative nature of your skill development, as you both contribute to your understanding of a task.

DEVELOPING YOUR EMOTIONAL INTELLIGENCE

Emotional intelligence is the understanding of your self. An element of emotional intelligence is an understanding of your strengths and areas for development, which is a theme throughout this book. It is also an understanding of the impact of yourself on others. Howe (2008) argues that in order to have empathy for a service user's position, you have to understand yourself and the impact your emotions can have on you so that you can understand how and why a service user may be reacting to you in a certain way. Ingram (2015) develops this further and recognises that social work is a complex ethical practice and that emotions, as well as personal and professional values, often impact on a social worker when they are balancing competing needs of the service user and/or agency to make a decision. He argues that an emotionally intelligent social worker is not one who tries to supress such emotions, but instead is the social worker who reflects upon how their emotions and values impact upon their decision making and service provision.

Kwan and Reupert (2019) support this view and recommend reflective practice on the impact of personal experience on social work intervention. As a social work student, you will be expected to reflect on such matters verbally in supervision and in written reflections, and these ideas can usefully be read in conjunction with Chapter 6.

Additionally, emotional intelligence is an understanding of who you are and the influences that shape who you are. You will be influenced by your life experiences, cultural experiences and educational experiences. Tedam's (2012) MANDELA model (see Chapter 4) argues that a practice educator should discuss with a student of black-African heritage how their cultural and educational experiences impact on their ability to engage with learning activities, but this can be embraced by all students. Consider what has made you the student that you are and how it influences your decision making, reactions and values. This emotionally aware approach will start to enhance your skill development.

....

POTENTIAL PLACEMENT *PITFALL* Blessing is a black Zimbabwean student whose cultural experiences have taught her to be deferential to a teacher. She is very capable of following directions, but struggles to show initiative within decision making. Her practice educator tells her that she needs to be proactive, but she finds this difficult, and concerns escalate as she remains unaware of the need to reflect on her perspective.

POTENTIAL PLACEMENT *OPPORTUNITY* Beauty is a black Zimbabwean student whose cultural experiences have taught her to be deferential to a teacher. She is very capable of following directions, but struggles to show initiative within decision making. Her practice educator tells her that she needs to be proactive, and explores with her the reasons why she finds this difficult. Whilst at first such a challenge to her cultural heritage is difficult, Beauty reflects and is able to recognise that social work necessitates decision making and, with the practice educator's help, starts to develop her confidence in her ability to make decisions.

....

Furthermore, remember that life happens to us all, and it is inevitable that some students will experience personal difficulties (e.g. debt, relationship breakdown, bereavement or health issues) during placement. Ferguson (2018) argues that the self is not limitless, but instead is sometimes *defended* by social workers in difficult interventions to protect their wellbeing. He argues that this in the short term is a healthy coping strategy, but that reflection on action and discussion in supervision to acknowledge and understand the impact of your self on your intervention skills is necessary to ensure that it does not become a long-term coping strategy at the expense of analysis and assessment of the service user's needs.

It is important to realise that short-term stressors (e.g. lack of sleep, an argument with your partner) can impact negatively on your intervention with a service user. Beesley et al. (2018) remind us that a barrier to listening to a service user can be anxiety about a personal or professional issue.

If you are emotionally intelligent and can recognise the impact of your self on your practice, you will be able to engage your practice educator in a productive manner. Edmondson (2014: 166) uses the acronym TALK to remind us to **T**ell those involved what is happening, **A**ccept the different perspectives of others, **L**isten to those perspectives and **K**now when a problem is impacting on your practice. He makes a good point. As placement progresses it will become increasingly difficult to practice to the best of your ability if you are experiencing personal difficulties. It is imperative that you talk to your practice educator so that they can support you to address the difficulties and enhance your practice, and ultimately be successful in your placement. A practice educator will always be happier with an emotionally intelligent student social worker who shares the impact their life is having on them rather than a student who carries on stubbornly believing that they can 'work through it'. The practice educator will support you and adjust your learning opportunities if they understand you. This is not to say that you will have the expectations lowered, as you still need to meet professional standards, but instead that they will help you to reach those standards in an individualised way. Remember also that your tutor will be available to support you at such times. But informal support can be useful too. Flanagan and Wilson (2018) found that peer support was considered important to the student, mainly focusing on social media communication during placement, whilst Westwood (2019) and Cartwright (2017) reminds you of the need to remain vigilant to ethical issues of confidentiality when using social media.

Recognising that you need time off is critical as part of your professionalism, but in an assessed period can have significant impact. HCPC (2016) state that every professional should be fit to practice, and this includes health and stress levels. Being emotionally intelligent enough to be able to recognise when you are not fit to support a vulnerable service user is critical. A good mantra is only walk in the door of placement if you feel fit to be assessed.

DEVELOPING YOUR RESILIENCE

Whilst your placement should be a positive period of learning and development, it may also create stressful points. Activities such as mindfulness, meditation and yoga are all good ways to increase your ability to cope with day-to-day stress triggers, such as a long commute, so are positive activities for all social work students. Building your resilience, your emotional ability to respond positively to challenges and stressors, will enhance your ability to engage in learning opportunities on placement. Indeed, Palma-Garcia et al. (2018) found that the more resilient students were able to learn professional skills more effectively. Chapter 7 provides guidance to deal with constructive feedback and engage with your placement during a difficult period, but there can be other stressors on placement, for example a complex or demanding service user.

Greer (2016) reasons that social work is a stressful profession, and that protecting yourself from the impact of stress is a positive attribute. He argues that being a *resilient* social worker contributes to a longer career. He suggests that resilience is your ability to deal with stressful situations, arguing that self-confidence, self-efficacy, optimism and commitment are all successful contributors to your resilience. It is therefore important that as a social work student you understand yourself and recognise stress factors and respond with positivity to them. Becoming a social worker is not an easy process, you will need to be aware of when you are finding your learning journey difficult and be able to access appropriate support. Your practice educator will be, as discussed in Chapter 3, your educator, supporter, manager and assessor (ESMA) (Doel, 2010). Your first port of call should be to talk to your practice educator about how you are coping, ask for support and together develop coping strategies. This is not an easy task in a complex power dynamic. Greer (2016) suggests seeing challenges as learning opportunities, for example, developing your ability to express your feelings or be assertive, which will be discussed in greater depth in Chapter 7.

Reflective Task 1.4

How do you look after YOU?

What positive coping strategies do you have for dealing with stress?

Whilst you should consider the impact that stress has on you as an individual, as a learner and as a practioner, you should also be aware of your coping strategies to reduce and manage your stress levels. It is very hard being assessed for the whole period of a placement so you need to be at your most emotionally resilient during that time. It is simple but effective advice to find time for *you* whilst on placement. Burg et al. (2017) argue that when a person is stressed they are less likely to prioritise exercise, but that they are less likely to be stressed if they have exercised. It does not have to eat into your time-limited life – taking a lunch-break walk will improve your afternoon concentration on placement. There is also no harm in reminding you that eating and sleeping well can only enhance your emotional resilience and ability to learn. Similarly to Burg et al., Walid et al. (2014) found that eating healthy foods reduced stress levels and reduced stress levels resulted in healthy eating in university students. Greer (2016) would argue that a positive approach to diet and exercise reduces stress levels and increases your resilience to cope with a stressful period.

Heffer and Willoughby (2017) found that for university students facing stressful situations, a flexible range of coping strategies was productive, but that using positive coping strategies had better outcomes than negative coping strategies such as drinking alcohol to relax. They argued that positive coping strategies included positive thinking, developing self-esteem and academic achievement.

As a social work student, you should try to be the best that you can be. If you reflect on every experience, success and failure, you will be able to identify positives models of intervention that work well for you and the service user, whilst also recognising and avoiding repetition of strategies that have not been successful, to enable you to explore different ways of approaching complex situations that may result in different outcomes. Your resilience will strengthen as you recognise that you develop by making, acknowledging and learning from your mistakes and your confidence grows in your self.

▬▬▬ PLACEMENT PERSPECTIVE 1.2 ▬▬▬

Student perspective

In the absence of direct experience in a statutory social work setting prior to the commencement of a social work degree, you may not be sure if you want to work in children or adult social work. Be inquisitive, and you will be surprised to find out about the variety of social work roles. Shadow a social worker if it is an option. Seek volunteering and/or employment opportunities where you could use your social work skills. This will help you to gain your confidence, enhance your skills and apply your knowledge. Before you start your placement, reflect on your learning needs. Speak with your tutor, friends and family who know you well and will be open with you.

Seek feedback and do not hesitate to seek support from your tutor.

Once your placement has been confirmed, research relevant laws, policy and guidelines, social work theories and so on for your placement interview. Most importantly, show your enthusiasm in your interview. Once on placement, build contacts with other students in similar placements and talk to them if things get tough. If you receive constructive feedback, focus on what could have been done differently without criticising or blaming other people. It may not be easy, but it is vital in order to pass your placement.

Biraj Gurung, BA Social Work Student

CHAPTER SUMMARY

Learning on a social work placement is often the area that social work students look forward to, an opportunity to work with service users, practice skills and implement knowledge. This chapter contends that you must understand who you are as a learner in order to maximise your learning opportunities. The theme that will underpin this book is that commitment to learning and reflection on your skills will enable you to fulfil your potential as a social worker and to complete your placement successfully and positively.

CHAPTER CHECKLIST

In order to maximise your understanding of your developmental needs, and to complete the task effectively and efficiently, ensure that you:

✔ reflect on both your strengths and areas for development before and during placement
✔ develop coping strategies to support you before placement to enhance your ability to engage with learning opportunities in placement
✔ be proactive in addressing learning needs throughout placement
✔ represent yourself positively within all placement procedures
✔ develop your emotional intelligence to be able to recognise when stress levels are impacting on your practice.

■■■ Further reading ■■■

Doel, M. (2010) *Social Work Placements: A Traveller's Guide*. Oxford: Routledge.

Chapter 3 'Making sense of yourself as a learner', in Fenge, L., Howe, K., Hughes, M. and Thomas, G. (2014) *The Social Work Portfolio: A Student's Guide to Evidencing your Practice*. Maidenhead: Open University Press.

Greer, J. (2016) *Resilience and Personal Effectiveness for Social Workers*. London: SAGE.

Greetham, B. (2018) *How to Write Better Essays*. London: Palgrave.

2

FULFILLING THE UNIVERSITY PROCESS WITHIN A PLACEMENT

This chapter will support the social work student to understand how to successfully engage with the university processes that frame the placement and assess the student. It will work through the placement process and address how to successfully complete the placement application form, informal meeting, placement learning agreement meeting, direct observation, interim and final report and meeting. The remit here is to maximise learning through each procedure.

■■■■■ PLACEMENT PERSPECTIVE 2.1 ■■■■■

Practice educator's perspective on the processes that a social work student completes on placement

The placement handbook is valuable tool for students, as it contains all the processes and expectations of the student both prior to and during the practice learning opportunity. It is empowering for students as it contains both the expectations of the student and the expectations the student should have of me as the practice educator.

The placement application form (PAF) is the first document that I receive about my student, and even at this stage I am already beginning my assessment of that student's practice. If I receive a PAF that is well written it will reassure me that a student might be competent to write, with support and advice, assessments, reports and case notes.

Written documents in any form can and will be shared with service users, so it is important that they are consistently of a high quality. The PAF is also the first document I receive that tells me about a student's existing experience and learning needs, and as such this allows me to begin to plan work for the student on the placement.

I always look forward to my first meeting with a student prior to the placement commencing. In this meeting I am hoping that the student has prepared and is presentable, almost as though they are attending a job interview. I am assessing how much information the student has gathered about the placement before the meeting and am hoping to be asked relevant questions both about

(Continued)

practical aspects of the placement such as parking and local amenities as well as questions relating to the work that they will undertake on the placement.

As a practice educator I am assessing a student's ability to reflect across a range of experiences on placement, both written and in supervision. I am interested in how they feel and am keen to explore any anxieties a student has. I want to support them to make sense of their feelings in respect of what they have seen and heard, and develop strategies for coping with similar situations better in the future. Reflection helps in the process of building up emotional resilience, which is an important skill for a social worker.

My advice to a student preparing for a direct observation would be not only to prepare for

the interaction with the service user but to also spend some time reflecting on their own feelings about having their practice observed. Really think about the objectives you are hoping to achieve with the service user. I would always advise a student to spend time writing a plan of questions. These do not have to be prescriptive but can act as a prompt to guide you during the observation. This is important because you are experiencing the added pressure of being observed, and this can help keep you on track. Don't panic, you will receive feedback on the observation which will help you to reflect and improve your practice in the future.

Sarah Taylor, Practice Educator

PLACEMENT PROCESS

Flanagan and Wilson (2018) found that 90% of social work students were satisfied or very satisfied with their placement, most learnt more than they had expected to, and it was seen as a very important part of social work education and development by most social work students. They argue that social work students often underestimated how prepared they needed to be to start placement, and many students noted that in retrospect they wish that they had started placement with more relevant knowledge in the placement.

Every student on a social work placement will have to follow and successfully complete a proscribed university process. Your university will provide, often in the form of a placement handbook supported with in-lecture explanations, clear detail of what you need to do and when. It is time well spent to familiarise yourself with these expectations, as failure to undertake a process can be catastrophic.

....

POTENTIAL PLACEMENT *PITFALL* Lorna receives her prospective placement offer and feels that she 'knows what she's doing', so does not look at her placement handbook. Unfortunately, as a result she does not contact her practice educator in good time, and the placement offer expires. She now has to wait for a second placement opportunity to be allocated to her, and she starts placement late. By consequently finishing placement late, she misses the opportunity to work on Camp America that summer, a life-long dream.

POTENTIAL PLACEMENT *OPPORTUNITY* Hannah receives her prospective placement offer and, having read the placement handbook, knows what she should do next. She contacts and visits the placement, which accepts her.

....

Whilst every university will have their own timescale and even names for different points in the placement, there is a common process that each student will follow, as demonstrated in Figure 2.1.

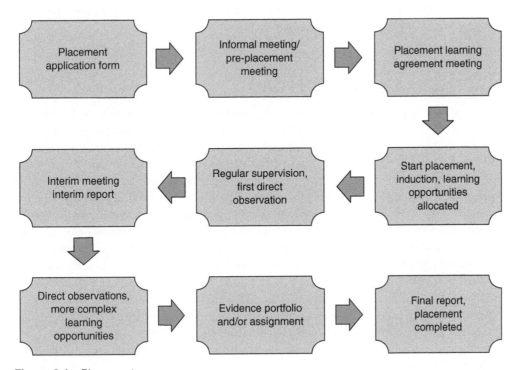

Figure 2.1   Placement process

The placement process is there to ensure a consistent and quality placement for you, and to give you boundaries to work within and towards. It is also there to protect you should placement not go as planned. However, it is also an opportunity at every stage to demonstrate your organisational skills, commitment and social work skills. As with all elements of placement, you only get as much out as you put into learning opportunities. If you engage with enthusiasm and commitment you are likely to learn new skills, understand the theory underpinning your intervention, and make a good impression with your practice educator or co-worker. As you progress through this chapter, you will be asked to reflect on how you can best represent yourself at each stage, thereby enhancing your ability to pass placement, but more importantly will enhance your skills in preparation for your post-qualification career.

The university may ask you for your placement preference. This may be a simple choice between an adults or childrens placement, which would encourage thought as to where your career preferences are, or a factual choice such as geographical preference between two areas. However, it may also include a more detailed service user preference, which can be rife with pitfalls such as raising your expectations for a non-existent placement provider or creating competitive placement applications. Cooper (2010) reminds us that placement demand always outstrips availability, and to be realistic in expectation. As a rule of thumb, it is better to express a generic interest than a very detailed one. A placement provider can be discouraged to accept a strong student who has preferenced a clear and specific service user group whom they do not want to work with. At this stage, an open mind towards placement is critical, as all placement providers offer relevant and challenging learning opportunities.

PLACEMENT APPLICATION FORM

As a social work student, you will be expected to undertake two placements in social work settings, and the first task is to apply for a placement. Whilst this has some similarities to applying for a job, in that you need to represent yourself in a positive light to ensure that the placement provider can see your potential, it is different as it is not competitive and it should also be reflective, demonstrating that you have considered what you wish to learn from the placement. In order to apply for the placement, your university will ask you to complete a placement application form (PAF). A PAF will have different headings, dependent on your university's paperwork, but may have core themes to address, for example personal details, strengths and areas for development, and previous experience. Throughout each theme, take time to reflect on your personal and professional perspective. The PAF should be a personalised reflection of your learning needs and skills.

> Using a contemplative approach will help you to recognise and evidence your existing abilities … The way in which you complete this should aim to open up your opportunities by stating your knowledge, skills, attributes, experience and learning needs. (Jones, 2015: 16–17)

Personal details

This section should be a straightforward completion of a series of questions. It may include factual details such as date of birth, address and if you are a car driver. However, it may also include more complex questions.

Reflective Task 2.1

Do you have any personal issues that your placement will need to know about?

Have you maximised problem solving to minimise this?

How will you represent this issue in your PAF?

The first thing you need to do is have an open and honest conversation with the loved ones in your life. You are committing to a full-time job (be that five days a week in placement, or fewer days in placement combined with the rest of the week in university) and you will have study commitments in addition to this. You may have work commitments (let's be honest, students need to work to fund their university fees and living expenses), childcare, family or caring commitments, or even a social life. Benner and Curl (2018) found that social work students who worked alongside their studies were more likely to reach burnout than those who did not work, so ensure that you have support and healthy coping strategies to help you during this time.

Your social work placement will need to take priority for the duration. You will need to be available during office hours, so anticipate 8.30 am–5.00 pm, and allocate travel time. Consider now how this will impact on childcare or job commitments, then you will avoid difficulties later. That is not to say that if your child is ill in an emergency you cannot take the time off placement, but you will need to have daily routines covered. By having addressed this before writing your PAF, you can honestly reflect that you have cover but that it may impact in exceptional circumstances, which will impress your placement provider as being organised and reflective.

Similarly, if you have a health or disability need, it is better to disclose it at this point. The placement should make reasonable adjustments to facilitate your learning wherever possible. It is your legal right to choose not to do so, but you cannot later complain that the placement did not meet your needs if they were not aware of them. Your tutor and placement co-ordinator will match your declared needs and will negotiate a suitable placement to ensure that your learning needs are met. The reflection that you undertake now to enhance your placement experience is a critical foundation to the success of your placement. Hunt and Matthews (2018) remind us that such issues can be aggravated by the rigours of a social work placement, and that honesty is always the better route.

POTENTIAL PLACEMENT *PITFALL* Anisa has a child who needs monthly hospital visits, but does not feel it is relevant as it is not about her, so she does not refer to it in her PAF or pre-placement meetings. Once placement starts she begins to ring in sick one morning a month, and the practice educator becomes concerned and raises the matter.

POTENTIAL PLACEMENT *OPPORTUNITY* Isabelle has a child who needs monthly hospital visits and discusses it with her practice educator and tutor, offering solutions that enable her to complete her placement with minimum impact. She is praised for her organised and reflective preparation for placement.

One final area that may be addressed in this section of your PAF is your disclosure and disbarring service (DBS). Whilst your DBS may be clear, a number of students have warnings and offences on their record. Again, a philosophy of an open and honest approach to this is best. A reflective account that shows learning from the incident will address any concerns that a placement provider may have. Many universities address this at the beginning of the course and will not require you to repeat this process at PAF stage, but be aware of your university procedure so that you are prepared if necessary.

Strengths and areas for development

You may be asked to reflect on your strengths and skills and reflect on the skills that you would like to and/or need to develop in your prospective placement. It will be very important to show that you are open to learning. Going through your placement assessment criteria (i.e. PCF, KSS, SOPs) can aid your understanding, and Chapter 1 discusses considering your strengths and areas for development.

If you have an assessed learning need, it is beneficial before and during placement to develop coping strategies that enable you to complete the expected placement tasks. Your university will offer individual and group tutorials and e-learning on these skills – make use of them. Your practice educator will help you to develop coping strategies to manage your practice learning opportunities. For example, Hunt and Matthews (2018) provide excellent advice to practice educators on how to support a student with dyslexia. Working together to ensure that you achieve the required level of capability will be critical to your success.

Previous experience

When writing the section in your PAF on your previous experience, practice your concise but clear writing skills and ensure that you keep focus on the PAF criteria. You need to supply your placement provider with a summary of your personal and professional experience, which can include personal caring or life experiences as well as voluntary, placement and work experience. It is important that you recognise transferable skills, for example developing communication skills and conflict management skills when dealing with difficult customers if you worked in a bar; and value life experience, such as the development of your understanding of diversity through the cultural immersion of back-packing in Asia or the organisational skills required to be a parent. It is equally important to share relevant work experience in social care settings where you may have developed, for example, empathic skills.

However, the potential placement provider does not want to wade through pages of description, so ensure that you briefly and concisely outline the skills that you learnt from the experience. A common acronym is KISS: keep it short and simple – a good mantra (source unknown). If your tendency is to write excessively, or to describe in detail, then now is the time to start to address this area of development. Case notes and reflections also require brevity whilst covering all pertinent points, so it is a skill worth developing. Greetham (2018) advocates that time spent choosing the correct word to represent your meaning is worthy, rather than settling for an approximation.

> **Reflective Task 2.2**

In 200 words summarise your previous work and life experience concisely.

REVIEW OF YOUR PAF

Doel (2010) reminds us that late PAFs may be allocated placements after timely PAFs, so allow time for proofreading, tutor checking and further alterations. If you use as a simple rule of thumb 'Does this PAF represent me in the way I wish to be seen?', then this technique will quality-assure your PAF before it is seen by a placement provider.

POTENTIAL PLACEMENT *PITFALL* A practice educator reads a PAF and is concerned that the level of grammatical errors and spelling mistakes as this implies that the student will struggle to write reports, assessments and case recording to the agency expected level. He is reluctant to invite the student to informal interview stage. He does invite the student to placement, but she finds it a challenging interview as he questions her writing skills, which she has always prided herself on.

POTENTIAL PLACEMENT *OPPORTUNITY* A practice educator reads a PAF and is impressed with its clear concise written style. He feels confident that the student will, with support, be able to write documents in placement, and invites the student to an informal interview.

This simple mistake is often made by students who feel pressurised to complete the PAF in a hurry, or who fail to see the importance of it at this early stage of placement preparation as it can be written six months in advance. Write your PAF as described above, then leave it for at least 24 hours, by which time you should be able to proofread and enhance your first draft. Greetham (2018) argues that you must transfer your thinking from writer to editor, and read it neutrally to ensure that it represents you as you hoped.

INFORMAL/PRE-PLACEMENT MEETING

Once the practice educator has agreed to consider you for their placement, you will be asked to contact them. *Do so immediately.* This is your second chance to make a first impression, so a timely and enthusiastic response will demonstrate your commitment to placement.

My best advice to students at this point is keep trying to contact the practice educator if you do not get an immediate response. It is *your* responsibility to contact them, and social workers can be elusive creatures who mean to ring you back but get side-tracked with a crisis.

Arrange a mutually convenient meeting time and ensure that you have the correct address to attend. The practice educator is likely to want to assess your interest in their placement and knowledge of the service user group. Arendt (2015) argues that knowledge of your future agency is critical for a successful social work job interview. Preparation spent in researching this will be invaluable, as it both impresses the practice educator and enhances your initial knowledge of the service area, starting to meet domains five (knowledge) and eight (contexts and organisations), making starting placement easier to navigate. Arendt also recommends knowing yourself, so continue the reflection on your strengths and areas for development that you began in Chapter 1.

The commonly asked questions in Reflective Task 2.3 indicate that by reflecting on your responses you will enhance your informal meeting performance.

Reflective Task 2.3

Imagine that you have been allocated a placement in a child protection team or community mental health team. Answer the following questions:

Why do you feel that this will be a positive placement for you?

What skills will you bring to this placement?

What do you want to learn whilst on this placement?

What do you feel is the relevant legislation or theory that will apply to this placement?

What do you want to know about this placement?

None of these are difficult questions. They should be areas that you have already addressed in your social work teaching, but when put on the spot without preparation can leave you tongue-tied and dry-mouthed. Feiler and Powell (2016) undertook research into the impact of anxiety on interview performance and identified that positive interpersonal skills mitigated nerves. Given that a core social work skill is that of communication, it is clear that the ability to engage the practice educator will enhance the meeting. Rook (2013) recommend succinct responses that focus on one's strengths and transferable skills. Practice educators are not looking for complex answers – you are there to learn after all – but instead will be assessing your interest and commitment.

Schmidt et al. (2018) argue that positive feedback on interview strategies can enhance your future interview performance, so undertake Reflective Task 2.3 with a peer from the course, and ask them to give positive feedback. This should boost your self-confidence, self-esteem and positive approach to the informal meeting. Arendt (2015) reminds us that this is your opportunity to discover what the team and agency are like, so do not forget to ask for the information that you want about the placement.

PLACEMENT LEARNING AGREEMENT MEETING

The placement learning agreement (PLA) meeting is arranged after a successful informal/pre-placement meeting, and should include yourself, your practice educator and your tutor. Most universities will expect you to arrange this meeting. This might be the hardest task of your placement, as trying to co-ordinate busy diaries often with short notice can be challenging, so undertake this task promptly. The best method is usually an email to all meeting participants with a number of possible dates, which can be a starting point for negotiation.

The university may have provided you with a PLA form, so ensure that you have printed and read it in preparation for the meeting. The PLA meeting agenda will follow the PLA form, which may cover a number of different areas: contact details, your learning needs, the placement learning opportunities and expectations, and assessment requirements. Many universities ask the student to complete it – another early task where the practice educator will assess your organisational skills. Frith and Martin (2015) argue that good meeting minutes concisely summarise the discussion and remind participants of their agreed responsibilities. Contributing to and minuting meetings is a regular task for social workers, so you are already developing your skills such as note taking and completing forms for placement tasks. Ask the tutor for help or advice if you need to before the meeting.

Reflective Task 2.4

In a small group, undertake a mock PLA meeting. One person should volunteer to chair and contribute to the meeting by going through the PLA form and another should play the practice educator and answer questions, whilst you answer questions and takes notes on the form of your and others' responses.

Is this an easy task?

Can you keep pace with the discussion and take notes?

Can you read and understand your notes afterwards?

Is this a skill that you need to develop?

Effectively, the PLA form is a contract: it outlines what you can expect whilst on placement and what you are required to do. After the PLA meeting you may be required to type up the form and distribute it for approval before gathering signatures and adding the completed document to your evidence folder or send it your administrator, as directed by your placement handbook.

PRACTICE LEARNING OPPORTUNITIES

When starting a placement, you will undertake an induction. Edmondson (2014) emphasises the importance of the induction in terms of preparing you for your learning during the term of your placement. This will be an opportunity for you to understand where your placement fits in local service provision, the remit of the team in which you are placed, and get to know how the service operates. Whilst you may be given procedures and case notes to read, you will also be afforded the opportunity to shadow a variety of team members on a variety of visits. This is your opportunity to observe practice and reflect on how and why tasks are undertaken and to reflect on how you would consider undertaking the same task. This is the start of the collaborative learning process, with competent social workers modelling for you different styles of intervention. Discussion in supervision will be critical at this point as you start to reflect on yourself, as you begin to develop an awareness of your own social work identity. Bradley (2008) found that induction where the inductee's existing knowledge and learning needs were taken into account were the most effective, so ensure that you participate and self-advocate in shaping the induction.

As your induction completes, your practice educator will begin to allocate practice learning opportunities to you. This will be, depending on the agency requirements, a mix of co-working cases or taking the lead on a straightforward case, and may also include group work and project work. It will be carefully considered by the practice educator to enhance your existing skills and support you to develop new skills, and should be reviewed throughout the placement to ensure that your practice learning opportunities continue to challenge you without overwhelming you, and meet your learning needs. As discussed throughout the book, you will be required to embrace all practice learning opportunities with enthusiasm to maximise your learning.

DIRECT OBSERVATIONS

Every social work student is expected to be observed a minimum of three times on each social work placement. Direct observations can strike fear into the heart of any social worker, student to long-serving qualified social worker, so please understand that you may be anxious. However, assessment of you as a student is not a discrete activity that only occurs at direct observation points, but should be an ongoing process throughout placement. Stone (2018) found that social work students often became preoccupied with direct observation as the main source of assessment within their placement; remember that the practice educator will draw on a wider range of materials to assess you, including service user and colleague feedback, supervision and informal observation. Furthermore, direct observations are not a pass/fail that needs to be completed successfully, but an opportunity for your practice educator to observe your practice, assess your skills and offer constructive feedback to develop your skills further. In many ways they should form an opportunity for the practice educator to identify learning needs and plan for the remainder of the placement to support you to enhance your skills further.

All of that said, you still will want to do your best in your direct observation I am sure. It is the opportunity to showcase your skills, demonstrate how much you have developed within placement and illustrate your working relationships with service users. A successful direct observation is a well-planned and orchestrated event.

■■■■■■■ Tips to Consider when Planning a Direct Observation ■■■■■■■

- Plan an intervention that provides sufficient challenge and opportunity for you to showcase your skills, without being so complex that you are unable to achieve the task that you planned. Plan an intervention that has one clear task, and discuss it in advance with your practice educator to ensure that they feel it will be appropriate.
- You will need to put thought into which service user will be a good choice. Ensure

that you will have enough to talk about, and that they will participate, but neither of you dominate.

- Ensure that the direct observation has value and meaning for the service user too. Repeating yesterday's assessment to be observed after a practice run is not ethically acceptable.
- But do not limit yourself to the 'easy' service user who will agree with you throughout.

A good observation also reflects on your ability to respond to challenge.

- You will require the service user's informed consent to be observed prior to the intervention. Mathews et al. (2014) remind us that a power imbalance exists between yourself and the service user, however powerless you may feel as the assessed student. You have an ethical duty to consider the service user's capacity to agree to the observation. This means that you will need to consider not only if they can give informed consent, but also that your role does not unwittingly force them to agree to seek your approval.
- Consider the time, date and location of the direct observation, consulting observer and service user availability and suitability.

POTENTIAL PLACEMENT *PITFALL*

DIRECT OBSERVATION 1 Nanjeep was anxious about being observed. As a naturally quiet student, for his first direct observation he felt it best to plan a written, reflective activity with the service user, and was able to support the service user to complete it effectively. However, the practice educator feedback said that she had been unable to assess his communication skills as the service user and he had spoken infrequently after he had introduced the task.

DIRECT OBSERVATION 2 As a result, in his second direct observation Nanjeep organised a two-hour session where he and the service user undertook a risk assessment, created a support plan, discussed housing, employment and recreational needs, and phoned services together. However, the practice educator feedback said that Nanjeep had not recognised the service user's exhaustion after an hour, and had not had time to complete any task effectively

POTENTIAL PLACEMENT *OPPORTUNITY*

DIRECT OBSERVATION 1 Omar was anxious about being observed. However, he was able to work through the planned assessment visit effectively using the proforma as an agenda, and his practice educator gave him positive feedback about his organisational skills and respect for the service user, but asked him to develop his assertive communication skills.

DIRECT OBSERVATION 2 As a result, in his second direct observation Omar organised to complete a support plan with the service user. He ensured that he was clear about the remit of the visit and the agency's resources. His practice educator praised his clear communication.

In the first example, Nanjeep was trying so hard to do what he thought was right for his assessment that he forgot to think about the service user's needs. Beesley et al. (2018) discuss that a barrier to listening to the service user can be due to anxiety about one's performance or the need to meet a criterion. Reflect on how you will ensure that the service user remains at the centre of the intervention.

After your direct observation, you will receive feedback. You should receive verbal feedback on the same day as the observation and written feedback within a week. Race (2007) reflects that feedback is only effective for students if it is immediate, as the event referred to needs to be in your recent memory. If you do not receive timely feedback, you have the right to request it.

Alongside your observer's feedback, you should also undertake a self-evaluation of your practice. A critical part of emotional intelligence is developing your own self-awareness. Allocate some time to consider the areas that you feel went well, and those where you could enhance your skills. Prepare for your next supervision by identifying if there are learning needs that you have noted that require your practice educator's input with additional resources, direction or experiences. Whilst your practice educator and yourself may not identify identical evaluation, the differences and similarities in feedback will create an excellent starting point for a constructive discussion on maximising your learning from the direct observation.

Do not worry if you make a mistake in the direct observation. It is not the mistake that passes or fails placement, but the way you respond to it. If you are able take the constructive feedback and enhance your practice, not only will you go on to pass placement, but you will also have developed resilience skills along with the critiqued skills you go on to develop. However, if you choose to ignore the feedback, or worse, be belligerent about it, you are less likely to pass your placement and will stunt your own skill development. Chapter 7 discusses this further.

INTERIM/MID-WAY REPORT AND MEETING

The interim (sometimes known as mid-way) meeting is a chance for student, practice educator and tutor to reflect on your progress in placement, which you should be prepared to comment on by reflecting before the meeting.

Reflective Task 2.5

Reflect on your placement so far and identify the following.

- What is the best learning activity that you have experienced?

  o Describe briefly the activity.
  o Describe the learning from it.
  o What are your learning needs from it?

- What activity has challenged you the most?

  o Describe briefly the activity.
  o What did you find challenging about it?
  o What did you identify that you need to develop from it?

- What else do you wish to learn in the remaining time?

These are questions that you will frequently be asked at the interim meeting. By providing reflective responses, the practice educator will be able to assess your progress through placement. This task will also highlight if there are domains that you have not yet begun to meet, which will enable yourself and your practice educator to plan activities for the second half of placement. The practice educator will be asked their perspective on your progress, but you should be aware of your progress within placement before the interim meeting. Additionally, the tutor may review your learning needs from the PLA meeting and summarise any ongoing learning needs.

The interim (or mid-way) report will be written to reflect your progress. Whilst most universities ask the practice educator to write this, students are often required to contribute to it at some level. For those asked for the provision of evidence, please see Chapter 8 for guidance, whilst those asked to write about their development against each domain should consider this task as providing a series of short concise summaries and it will reduce your anxiety at this often daunting task. The draft interim report should inform the discussion at the interim meeting, but be finalised after the interim meeting with any additional discussion. To complete it you should circulate it for signatures and add it to your evidence folder (or email it to a nominated person) on completion.

FINAL REPORT AND MEETING

Many universities no longer hold a final meeting, unless there is a specific issue such as progress to discuss. Nevertheless, it is good practice for yourself and your practice educator (and practice supervisor if you have one) to review your development in each domain and learning needs for your next placement or first post-qualification job, whilst also planning endings and handovers for your service user interventions.

The practice educator should write your final report making a clear recommendation of your capability to meet and future learning needs for each domain.

■■■■■■■■■■ PLACEMENT PERSPECTIVE 2.2 ■■■■■■■■■■

Student's experience of completing university processes on placement

Completing the paperwork is good practice for when you qualify. Do it early and don't leave it to the last minute, because if not done properly it will affect your ability to pass your placement.

Prior to your placement meeting(s) do as much research as you can on the placement and service user group, and treat the initial meeting as a job interview. Use your practice learning agreement meeting as a way of practicing chairing a meeting.

Getting your head around appraising your own learning needs, as this is important and must be done early as your practice educator will

(Continued)

want you to bring your ideas to supervision. In the past I didn't promote the work I was doing as I felt it may come across as showing off or boasting. However, on placement you have to show off (within reason) by being aware of your strengths and how you have met a PCF domain. If something was challenging, openly discuss it in supervision. It is important to use your supervision to seek advice and feedback.

Within reflections you can start to think about your identity as a social worker, start to apply theories to yourself as well as to service users, and be honest about how you felt and why. Anything that produces tension in you whilst on placement should be written down as a reflection. I began to understand the wider context of decisions and I developed a more nuanced view. It is important to follow the structure of a reflective cycle, as this keeps you from ranting!

Prior to being observed, it is vital you seek permission from the service user. Direct observations can be nerve-racking; remember there is no rigid correct way of interacting with service users, so just be yourself and make sure you focus on the task at hand and the service user you are working with. It is important to direct what you are saying to the service user whilst being observed, not to your practice educator. Finally, it is easy to have a negative mindset and become self-conscious when something challenging happens whilst being observed. However, when you overcome them, they are often the times when you learn the most about your progress.

Hugo MacDonald-Hull, BA Social Work Student

CHAPTER SUMMARY

To reiterate: the more you put into placement, the more you will get out of it. Lomax and Jones (2014) remind us that you need to be proactive in your learning and accessing the learning opportunities. Your practice educator needs to see, at every stage of the placement process, that you are committed and enthusiastic about their placement and your learning. In order to complete your placement, you have to engage with these placement processes, but in order to enhance your learning you have to reflect on your skills and areas for development at every stage too.

CHAPTER CHECKLIST

In order to maximise your understanding of your developmental needs, and to complete the task effectively and efficiently, ensure that you:

✔ reflect on both your strengths and areas for development before and during placement
✔ be proactive in addressing organisational issues and learning needs throughout placement
✔ represent yourself positively within all placement procedures
✔ complete all tasks within the university requested timescale.

Further reading

Edmondson, D. (2014) *Social Work Practice Learning: A Student Guide*. London: SAGE.

Jones, S. (2015) *Social Work Practice Placements*. London: SAGE.

Lomax, R. and Jones, K. (2014) *Surviving your Social Work Placement*. London: Palgrave Macmillan.

Matthews, I., Simpson, D. and Crawford, K. (2014) *Your Social Work Practice Placement: From Start to Finish*. London: SAGE.

3

ESTABLISHING A RELATIONSHIP WITH YOUR PRACTICE EDUCATOR

This chapter will reflect on how to establish and develop a positive and collaborative working relationship when the practice educator is both your mentor and your assessor, and will contemplate professional boundaries. It will consider different aspects of supervision and how to use supervision to support your development.

━━━━━━━━━━━━ **PLACEMENT PERSPECTIVE 3.1** ━━━━━━━━━━━━

Practice educator expectations of a social work student relationship

When first meeting a social work student, I am interested in their motivation and enthusiasm for the role. I want to know why they want to become a social worker, which I expect to be reflective of them as a person and a professional. I find it helpful if they have life or work experiences or to have been in a caring/voluntary role, as this enables the student to have an understanding of situations.

To get the most from a placement, the social work student needs to be a team player as they will gain a lot of support and guidance from the social workers within the team. In supervision I expect the student to listen; there will be a reason for the practice educator asking for the task to be undertaken. I like a student who is inquisitive and wants to understand. I need them to consider

theory in their practice, to look at what they did and why they did it this way. I want to see them reflect on their values, question themselves why they thought that way.

Once on placement, I feel that the big aspirations for a social work student on placement should be to demonstrate the skills of time management, being proactive and have good communication skills. I always discuss and set tasks in supervision, and will review their completion to assess their time management skills. I cannot stress enough how important this is as completing tasks in time values service users and meets agency timescales. A social work student needs to be able to use their initiative and work autonomously whilst also demonstrating accountability by asking questions and actively

(Continued)

listening to further their understanding, even if they think the question is a stupid one to ask. Good verbal and written communication and interpersonal skills are essential to any form of social work practice; the student needs to be flexible in a wide range of interventions from making a telephone call to dealing with a complex situation with service user, carer and multiple professionals.

Throughout their placement I would also expect to see the social work student develop their emotional intelligence and deal with the stress of the role. A social work student needs to develop the ability to have empathy for the service user or carer they are working with to understand them. I would assess the social work student's self-awareness of the impact on a service user of how they dress, their verbal and non-verbal communication style and their ability to understand professional boundaries. I would expect a student to accept constructive feedback, be able to reflect on its content and use it to improve their practice.

Overall, I would expect to see an enthusiastic social work student who tries hard in all areas of practice and reflects on their practice to develop their growth and understanding of their practice.

Julie Roome, Practice Educator

ESTABLISHING A WORKING RELATIONSHIP WITH YOUR PRACTICE EDUCATOR

Developing a good working relationship is a critical contributor to the success of your social work placement. Research by Miehls et al. (2013) identified that social work students benefitted from a clear mentor relationship of mutual respect and partnership. When you first meet your practice educator, it is likely that you may feel a mixture of excitement, nervousness, eagerness and being daunted. They will become a significant person in your life for a short period, and a good practice educator can become a significant influence on you as a student and be remembered fondly for years. Remember that they are likely to be anxious too: they want to work with you to enhance your skills and may be anxious about letting you down. Have faith, a good working relationship can develop and be influential in your development. A good working relationship with your practice educator will facilitate collaborative developmental discussions that demand you reflect on different aspects of your understanding of your interventions, and enhance your skills, knowledge and values. Doel (2018) reminds the practice educator of the joy of new eyes seeing different perspectives and questioning long-held habits.

Some social work students will experience learning where the practice educator does not work in the office – an off-site practice educator (OSPE). If this is the case you will be allocated an in-office practice supervisor, and the two will divide the roles between them, agreed within the PLA meeting, which it will be important for you to understand. It is recognised that your relationship will be different with an OSPE as you will see them less frequently, but they are usually skilled and experienced practice educators who will be equipped to engage you quickly.

You will meet your practice educator at your pre-placement meetings, when they will assess your potential suitability and you will be seeking information about your prospective placement. Be prepared to try to fit into agency hours wherever possible. Kay and Curington (2018) found that whilst most practice educators would be flexible in theory, this was often restricted by agency demands. As discussed in Chapter 2, the best way to engage your practice educator, and the best way to maximise your own learning in those meetings, is to present as organised and reflective, an emotionally intelligent social work student who is aware of their strengths and areas for development and personal learning needs will be well received.

As discussed in Chapter 2, if you have an individual learning need it is up to your practice educator to *support you* in this, but it is *your* responsibility to have coping strategies in place to support your development and therefore the ability to pass placement. If you know that a significant amount of information in one go can overwhelm you, ask to have smaller, more frequent information sessions to facilitate your learning. The practice educator will be impressed with your understanding of your learning needs and you will learn more productively. The more you can have open discussions and identify together your learning needs, the more productive the placement will be. This is *collaborative* learning, and will be discussed as this chapter develops.

When starting on placement, it is very difficult to get the correct balance of reserved but not shy, chatty but not loud, inquisitive but not ask too many questions, knowledgeable but not a know-it-all. The best advice is to 'be yourself'. Remember that social workers are skilled people assessors, and will quickly see through a false persona that is trying too hard. That said, the next reflection is a worthy one.

Reflective Task 3.1

Think back to your first day on your social work course. How did you feel? How did you act?

Thinking retrospectively: did that first day represent you well? Are you aware that your personality becomes quieter or louder when anxious? Ask others how you come across.

Spend some time reflecting on the person you are, and whether you need to adjust your initial presentation to engage people effectively. Being proactive in induction will enhance your learning opportunities. The team you are in will also play a significant role in your development and you may feel embraced or excluded by the team culture. If a common social bonding activity is a weekly after-work drink and you do not drink, or have commitments such as work or childcare that prevent you from engaging, then this may leave you alienated from the group. You might need to be creative to engage the team at a point that works for you and them, for example developing a lunchtime coffee and sandwich routine, because the support from the team will enhance your practice. Flanagan and Wilson (2018) found that team support enhanced students' understanding of the role and work, and Oliver et al. (2017) concluded that peer discussion to explore perspectives boosted the effectiveness of subsequent supervision discussion. Similarly, Atwal (2019) reminds us that team discussions are a fine method for reflection and case discussion. It is often in those informal team chats that you can explore how you are feeling and process ethical dilemmas by utilising the knowledge and breadth of experience within the team.

It can be daunting at first to have the confidence to do so, particularly if you are a quieter social work student. But even if your contributions are minimal, being part of the discussion will be invaluable in developing your understanding.

ROLE OF THE PRACTICE EDUCATOR

Roulston et al. (2018) found that supervision, induction observational visits, constructive feedback and reflection were the most important strategies to maximise learning from practical experiences within a social work placement. These are core roles for a practice educator, who should offer you a certain minimum level of support as outlined below, and most practice educators offer significantly more than that.

■ Role of the Practice Educator ■

- Attend informal introductory meeting and PLA meeting.
- Arrange induction programme, make practical arrangements to facilitate the placement and prepare team for your arrival.
- Offer a minimum of one and a half hours per week supervision, which can be a mix of formal and informal supervision.
- Monitor and manage your practice learning opportunities throughout the placement.
- Liaise with practice supervisor and/or team manager where appropriate.

- Liaise with tutor where appropriate.
- Undertake at least two of the minimum three direct observations, and facilitate direct observations undertaken by anyone else.
- Attend initial and final meetings, write interim and final reports.
- Gather service user feedback.
- Read and confirm evidence folder where appropriate.
- Co-mark academic assignment if university procedure.

As a student, you have a right to the practice educator's support and constructive feedback to help you to develop your skills, knowledge and values. If you feel that you are not getting a sufficient level of support, communication is key. First, raise your concerns with your practice educator, but if this does not resolve your concerns then you must discuss it with your tutor who will mediate. Nevertheless, it is worth remembering that a practice educator is also a social worker who will have a complex and demanding case load, and that sometimes you will need to have empathy for their needing to change commitments in the face of an emergency.

SUSTAINING A WORKING RELATIONSHIP WITH YOUR PRACTICE EDUCATOR

Once you have got into the rhythm of placement, you will have developed a working relationship with your practice educator, where you each understand the level of work that you can manage that appropriately challenges you and the level of support that your practice educator will provide to maximise your development. At this point your practice educator should be offering you regular supervision and be accessible within the team room between times. You may have the chance to co-work a case, which is a good opportunity for you to observe their practice. Bandura (1977) argued that *modelling* contributes to the outcome of a learner's ability, as the learner observes behaviour, attitudes and values from those important figures around them. Within a placement the practice educator plays a critical role in demonstrating good practice and creative interventions for you to observe, evaluate and emulate. Sennett (2008) proposes that a student learning a new skill benefits from *expressive instruction*, where reflective discussion enables the student's understanding to enhance their practice. He argues that mere modelling is insufficient for the student to observe and replicate the mentor's good practice. It becomes clear that your relationship with your practice educator is key to your developing skills. Your understanding of your practice will develop through collaborative discussion where you are each able to express your ideas and explore ethical dilemmas to identify the most appropriate intervention for the individual service user. Just as valuable is observing different styles of practice – reflect upon which you feel suits your social work professional style and will be most effective for you.

As the placement develops, your practice educator will assess your strengths and areas for development through observation, gathering feedback, discussion with you in supervision and reading your written work. Supervision will be most effective if you can identify your own strengths and areas for development and are open to reflective, constructive discussions that enhance your understanding of the work undertaken. This will enable your practice educator to allocate work that will develop your self-confidence, and challenge and stimulate you without overwhelming you. Vygotsky (1978) introduced the *zone of proximal development*, the gap between what a student can do and their potential ability to learn with support. The zone of proximal development can be seen to be the area that the practice educator will support you to progress through whilst on placement, the area between your ability and potential. The placement is a time for continual development, and no matter how well you feel that you are doing, you should be enthusiastically engaging with your practice educator so that you can work together to achieve this. Lomax and Jones (2014) urge the social work student to be proactive in their learning.

....

POTENTIAL PLACEMENT *PITFALL* Yasmin felt very safe with her practice educator. She was happy trusting her to direct her to learning opportunities, and always worked hard with positive outcomes for the service user. But her practice educator became concerned because Yasmin continued to rely on her for direction. She assessed that Yasmin lacked initiative and would struggle when making independent decisions as a qualified social worker.

POTENTIAL PLACEMENT *OPPORTUNITY* Rafi felt very safe with her practice educator. Initially she was happy trusting her to direct her to learning opportunities, and always worked hard with positive outcomes for the service user. However, as the placement progressed Rafi would make suggestions in supervision about work she could undertake, and by end of placement was able to make independent decisions by using her initiative.

....

At this point, good communication will be critical to your relationship with your practice educator. Beesley et al. (2018) consider that a good relationship with a service user is developed through good communication, and it is no different with your relationship with your practice educator. They advise that listening and empathy are important to understand the other person's perspective, and that clarification should be used to check mutual understanding. This is good advice for a supervisory relationship. Listening to your practice educator and clarifying that you understand the task asked of you will ensure that you undertake that task effectively and efficiently. Developing empathy skills so that you can understand your practice educator perspective will help you to understand why they are asking you to undertake tasks, and therefore be more committed to the task. Heron et al. (2015) argued that the nature of the practice educator/social work student relationship was key in the effectiveness of feedback, and therefore the success of the intervention and ultimately the placement. Good communication will enable you and your practice educator to understand each other, which will enhance both your individualised learning opportunity provision and your ability to engage with those learning opportunities.

You will also need to be aware of the personal and professional boundaries within your relationship with your practice educator. Whilst they are a team colleague, they cannot be your *friend*, as they are assessing you. You are not aiming to develop a relationship that sustains you outside of placement. Conversely, Edmondson (2014) reminds us that you may not like your practice educator, but that you still have to work with them professionally. Between you, you will need to negotiate a professional working relationship that enables a collaborative, open learning environment.

Many teams have cultural norms. Positive ones include stopping for lunch together, buddy system for difficult visits, or a traffic light system to indicate stress levels and the need for a cup of tea. Less positive cultural team norms can include working late each night, belittling colleagues or making jokes at a vulnerable service user's expense as a coping strategy. You will need to determine which of these you will adopt. It is too simple to state 'Just the positive ones, of course!'. You might feel pressure to be *one of the team* and begin to adopt less ethical habits. But remember that no relationship is worth breaking social work values and professionalism for, and at worst, whilst *you* are being assessed *you* can fail placement for such an attitude or behaviour.

POWER

As a social work student, it is likely that you will feel powerless at points in your placement because the practice educator assesses your practice and can wield the f-word (fail) at any point. It will be important that your practice educator treats you with respect and offers regular constructive feedback (as discussed in Chapter 7) to minimise the power differential. The student/practice educator relationship is a difficult one. The practice educator has to be mentor, educator and assessor, as well as a team colleague. This can cause blurred role definition and can be confusing for both parties. For example, it might feel difficult in supervision to shift from discussion about how you are feeling overwhelmed within placement into constructive feed-back on a difficult direct observation immediately afterwards. Egan et al. (2017) recognise that whilst a supervisor holds a position of power, this can be mitigated through respect, trust and support which facilitates a reflective dialogue in supervision. It is important that you discuss with your practice educator reflectively if you feel that this balance is not working for you at your earliest convenience – do not let it fester or it will become untenable. Remember that your tutor is also a good source of support and advice.

.... **Reflective Task 3.2**.......

Thinking back to your favoured learning styles in Chapter 1, how does this impact on your relationship with your practice educator?

Do you feel able to raise a lack of congruence with your practice educator if their supervision style does not match your learning need?

Can you think of a constructive way to phrase this so that it engages your practice educator and enhances your relationship?

You will need to be direct but subtle. Be clear in your meaning without offending your practice educator, and giving evidence-based examples can highlight your perspective. You need to ensure that you are able to assert your feelings clearly in an open and honest manner. This takes practice, but self-advocacy within a powerful relationship will be a critical skill for a social worker – one only has to observe professional hierarchies to understand this. Oliver et al. (2017) recognise the restrictions to a social work student challenging their practice educator as those of anxiety of a reaction, and lack of skills to advocate their perspective or challenge appropriately. They found that power imbalances were further impacted by identity differences, making it even harder to raise a different perspective. They argue that 'moral courage' can be developed through using your reflection to raise the issue you wish to discuss and preparing for supervision with a list of your arguments. Nevertheless, they were clear that the practice educator needed to be open to such a collaborative discussion within a safe space to empower the social work student to speak assertively.

It is inevitable that you and your practice educator will have some commonalities and some differences, and it is important that you acknowledge them together. Your practice educator will be committed to working in an anti-oppressive and anti-discriminatory manner. Tedam (2012) argues that social work students with a black-African heritage can be oppressed by their practice educator through lack of understanding and acknowledgement of the impact of their cultural heritage on their learning needs. She recommends that practice educators supervise with sensitivity, empowerment, encouragement and respect (SEER) to support students (Tedam, 2015). To engage with this and maximise your learning you should be open to exploration of the impact that your life, educational and cultural experiences have had on you and your learning style, which will enable you to work collaboratively to address the issues. Whilst the practice educator should be aware of the power differentials that these social and cultural differences can create, and ensure that they do not work in an oppressive manner towards and with you, that does not mean that you will not feel the oppression that is entrenched on a societal level. If you feel that this is the case you must, of course, raise it immediately with your tutor.

SUPERVISION

Supervision is a critical element of your social work practice placement learning. It will come in a variety of forms, both formal and informal supervision, and individual, group or peer supervision. It is where you reflect on the work that you have done and identify the theories that you may have used, or legislation and social policy that impacts upon your service user or service provision. You should be able to explore your values and reflect upon ethical dilemmas that occur within your practice learning opportunities. You will consider future intervention options, and ensure accountability for your work. Kuusisaari (2014) argues that collaborative work that neither completely agrees nor dismisses each other's ideas is the most productive in enhancing development. As the social work student, you should be able to hear the practice educator's perspectives and ideas, and question and clarify their meaning without fear of repercussion, to optimise outcomes for both student and practice educator. Indeed, Saltiel (2017) highlighted that the quality of supervision was dependent on a supervisor who enabled the social work student to reflect and explore their practice learning opportunities and barriers rather than offering definitive advice.

Reflective Task 3.3

What are your expectations for supervision?

What would you like to achieve in supervision? What would you like to gain from supervision?

Every student's supervision will be different, dependent on the student's learning needs, the student and the practice educator's learning styles, and the point in the placement. However, you should receive supervision that works for you and supports you to develop. In order to best access collaborative learning with your supervision, you should attend it prepared. Edmondson (2014) argues that your preparation is pivotal in effective supervision. First, you should be prepared with a list of the work that you have undertaken which ensures that you know each service user's intervention status, and be ready to seek clarification on future steps. Second, you should be prepared with any pre-reading or activity that has been requested of you. Third, you should be prepared to participate in the supervision. It is an active activity, so your contributions will be critical to its success.

Doel (2010: 102) identifies four functions of a practice educator within supervision, which he calls **ESMA: E**ducation, **S**upport, **M**anagement, **A**ssessment. It is your practice educator's responsibility to provide each of those areas, and it is your responsibility to engage with them.

Education

Initially, education will be focused on familiarising you with the placement processes. However, as placement progresses within supervision you will receive support and direction, which will then progress to you leading, on the theories, legislation and social policy that you will use in your interventions with service users. In order to maximise your learning and to demonstrate capability in all domains to your practice educator, you should attend supervision having read any agreed pre-reading, reflected on the area to be discussed, and developed a clear idea of where you want support with the knowledge to be shared.

Support

In every supervision, time should be afforded to discussing *you* and your emotional well-being. The practice educator should value your welfare, and recognise the impact that placement can have on you. Of course, the impetus is on you to be open and honest in sharing how you are coping and feeling so that the practice educator will be able to offer you appropriate support, which should ease the situation and enable you to practice to a higher standard, and inevitably be successful in placement.

Further to this, your practice educator should offer you constructive feedback on your progress and areas for development, along with support on how this can be achieved. In order to engage your practice educator, have a successful placement and maximise your learning from a mistake or area for development, you need to be open to feedback. Listen to and reflect on the practice educator's perspective, taking time if you need to process the information. Ask for and use support from your practice educator and other appropriate colleagues. But above all, indicate to your practice educator that you are open to addressing the concern and that you can learn from the feedback. Chapter 7 addresses this further.

Management

Within supervision, case management discussions are a non-negotiable stable of the agenda. The need for accountability has been made clear through every review of social work practice, including those of Laming (2003) and Munro (2017), and a social worker or student social worker who practices without due case management supervision is considered at risk of dangerous practice. You should attend supervision with an update of each of your practice learning opportunities, so that you can apprise your practice educator concisely and clearly of the case position, even where you are not the case holder. This will often result in the formulation of a 'to do' list for you to complete. This is not to say that the practice educator feels that you are incapable, but that it is part of the accountability role of management supervision to support and direct the future interventions. Nevertheless, timely completion of this list will be required to demonstrate your capability.

Assessment

Within every supervision, your practice educator will be assessing you. They will be analysing your responses, your reflections and your development as you progress throughout the placement. Knowing this, you should not be offended and instead calculate how to respond to maximise impact. This assessment should enable the practice educator to provide individualised education and support and management advice to enable you to practice most productively, completing the ESMA functions again.

POTENTIAL PLACEMENT *PITFALL* Geri did not value supervision. She wanted to 'do' social work, not talk about it. She tried to cancel supervision when she could, and attended without preparation for it. Her practice educator became frustrated at her reluctance to engage, which resulted in her practice educator assessing that Geri had a lack of interest in developing her social work knowledge and concerns were raised as a result.

POTENTIAL PLACEMENT *OPPORTUNITY* Emma and her practice educator booked supervision for the period of the placement and always prioritised it. She attended supervision with a clear agenda of what she wanted to discuss, which was amalgamated with the practice educator's agenda. Emma always had an up-to-date list of her practice learning opportunities, and queries that she needed clarifying. The practice educator enjoyed supervision discussions and always had new ideas to introduce and discuss.

You will need to demonstrate enthusiasm and organisational skills to collaboratively embrace the learning opportunities within supervision; this in turn will engage your practice educator who will see you as motivated and keen, and will be inspired to develop new areas with you. Jones (2015) argues that as a student, and indeed qualified social worker, one should always strive to enhance your knowledge and understanding, and that supervision enables you to explore these areas and boost your confidence and skills.

ENDING YOUR WORKING RELATIONSHIP WITH YOUR PRACTICE EDUCATOR

Just as important as establishing and sustaining your working relationship with your practice educator, is ending it. You will need to ensure that you complete all work required by your practice educator to enable transition or closure of cases, and you will need to think about the emotional impact of saying goodbye to your team. But first is often the provision of the evidence folder roughly two weeks before the end of placement, as discussed in Chapter 8. It is important to remember that this is your final chance to impress your practice educator, by demonstrating the breadth of work that you have undertaken whilst on placement as well as your development of skills from the work undertaken. Ensure that you agree a hand-in date for your evidence portfolio, and stick to it. This will require some planning and organisational skills, but if you follow the tips in Chapter 8 it is easily viable.

Your practice educator will want to have a final supervision that forms a handover of your workload, where you update each service user's position and needs. You may also review the placement. If you have reflected on this before supervision, you should try to offer your practice educator praise and constructive advice on how you have experienced the placement. This will enable future students' placements to be enhanced, and is also one final chance to be assessed as reflective. At this point, it can be easy to fall into the 'I've passed' trap. Be careful to ensure that your practice remains as committed as at the start of placement. Remember that you are assessed for every day that you are on placement, not just the first 95% of the placement days.

Then finally, you will reach the last day of placement. Your team might throw you a leaving lunch or buy you a small present. You may feel that you wish to buy your practice educator a small thank you present. Neither should be expected. Lomax and Jones (2014) remind us that it will be dependent on team culture and your individual placement experience. Nevertheless, what should be expected is a range of emotions, from relief and joy to finishing the placement, to the bereavement of leaving a good team or wonderful service users. As a social work student, you should be open to experiencing the range of emotions, and use them as a final learning opportunity: reflect on the learning from the placement and identify learning needs for future placement or qualified practice. If it has been a difficult placement experience for you, then there will be the chance to reflect and debrief, perhaps even the need to rebuild your confidence.

Reflective Task 3.4

How do you feel about goodbyes?

Are you able to move on objectively, or does it impact on you emotionally?

Begin to plan for the ending of your placement. An overly objective approach may imply a lack of investment in the placement, whilst an emotionally charged reaction may imply a lack of emotional resilience. Every placement activity can be seen as a learning event, and reflecting on your responses will enable you to identify future learning needs.

PLACEMENT PERSPECTIVE 3.2

Student perspective on relationship with their practice educator

For me, this was one of the most crucial relationships I had to develop because I wanted to pass placement but I also wanted to gain experience and knowledge from my practice educator. At first, I was apprehensive about meeting her, as I felt pressured and

(Continued)

overwhelmed with wanting to make sure I could a give a good impression. However, I found that my practice educator wanted to give me the best opportunities from my placement, which allowed me to be honest and comfortable around her, so I could express any concerns and ask for help in areas I felt less confident in. This allowed me to develop a positive relationship as well as a optimistic attitude during my time on placement. It is important to know that your practice educator is there to guide you, not judge you.

I found that it was important to take responsibility for my own development and actions while preparing for and being on placement. Do not be afraid to ask those questions you find awkward. Being on placement is a time when you should thrive the most because this is the only supported learning experience you will really get before becoming a social worker.

I found observations and regular supervision with my practice educator were a great way to discuss and review my practice, to gather an understanding of my capabilities and reflect together how I could progress further.

Deklon Brown, BA Student

CHAPTER SUMMARY

In conclusion, your relationship with your practice educator is pivotal to the success of your placement. Whilst you cannot control your practice educator's personality or caseload, you can influence their engagement with you. Remember that your practice educator will be committed to your learning, and that your enthusiasm, commitment and organisation will engage them further, whilst your disinterest or poor attitude will disengage them. Their engagement will influence both their provision of learning opportunities and your placement outcome, so is critical to your learning on placement.

CHAPTER CHECKLIST

In order to make the most of your relationship with your practice educator, which will ensure the best possible learning opportunities:

✔ spend time investing in developing a professional working relationship with your practice educator by using an open and honest communication style
✔ be yourself and yet be aware of the impact of yourself on others, as it will impact upon team and practice educator engagement
✔ prioritise supervision and attend with an organised and enthusiastic approach
✔ accept constructive feedback and developmental support with good grace and an open, reflective perspective
✔ address concerns raised by your practice educator expediently and with their help
✔ act professionally throughout your placement.

Further reading

Chapter 8 'Using supervision, reflective practice and critical thinking', in Edmondson, D. (2014) *Social Work Practice Learning: A Student Guide*. London: SAGE.

Chapter 4 'Working with your practice educator', in Fenge, L., Howe, K., Hughes, M. and Thomas, G. (2014) *The Social Work Portfolio: A Student's Guide to Evidencing your Practice*. Maidenhead: Open University Press.

Chapter 4 'Preparing for and using supervision', in Jones, S. (2015) *Social Work Practice Placements*. London: SAGE.

4

CULTIVATING A RELATIONSHIP WITH SERVICE USERS AND CARERS

This chapter will ask the student social worker to reflect on the importance of the service user (and carer) within their social work placement. It will focus on keeping the service user central to their learning and practice development. It will ask the student social worker to consider the impact of self on the service user, and will conclude with an exploration of gathering service user feedback.

━━━━━ PLACEMENT PERSPECTIVE 4.1 ━━━━━

Service users' perspectives on the importance of their relationship with a social work student

I always judge a social work student by whether I would welcome them into my home. A trusting relationship is so important; if I can't trust you I won't tell you half the things. Please do not judge me. I have sent for you as I am in distress. Treat me as an individual, we are not all the same. Please remember my culture, it is so important that you know I am different.

Be a good listener. Your communication skills as a whole should be very good. Relate to me that you have heard and will take action, I like you to show empathy. When you set goals, work together

with me to set them. Treat me and my family with respect. Support and empower me so that I can start to live a better life.

I expect professionalism. Always remember boundaries and confidentiality. If it will harm me or others that is fine, but only share with those who need to know. If I have relatives in my house, ask first before starting to talk to me in front of them.

At the end of a visit, ask if there is anything else I want to discuss, because it prompts me to help me remember. Give me time to think and answer.

(Continued)

As you are leaving, give me your contact details for the future.

Myrtle Oke, Service User

I started engaging with social work, social care and health care staff over twenty years ago, when I was a mental health social worker. I found this very hard because I knew what to expect, and was critical of the other professionals. I found that my knowledge initially got in the way of our communication, because they had to pitch it right: not too simple, but not too complex either, and they had to clarify that I had understood.

If a student social worker visits me in my house, I would expect respect. Always check where you can sit: I like to feel in control of where I sit so that I feel safe, or I will struggle to listen to you. If you cannot find a positive comment to say about my house, please do not say anything, as you need to engage me when we first meet. I expect you to have done some background information gathering: talk to the referrer and read case notes; but do not assume that it represents me. Please strike a balance of showing interest in my interests, but equally, keep me on track when I am talking.

Sometimes, you might feel that you have done nothing to help me, but listening to me can give me confidence, and make changes that you do not see. I want to be independent and feel positive; helping me to achieve that is very important to me.

Seonaid Matheson, Service User

THE MOST IMPORTANT FUNCTION OF BEING A SOCIAL WORKER

Arguably the most important part of becoming a social worker is your ability to engage a wide range of service users in a person-centred manner that meets their individual needs whilst working within the confines of the service requirements and boundaries. If you cannot engage the service user to assess their needs and provide appropriate support, you are likely to be ineffective as a social work student. For the purpose of this discussion, the term 'service user' will be used to refer to any adult, child or carer with whom you will work whilst on your social work placement, but it will be important for you to think about your service user individually, with respect for their cultural and individual needs. I would ask that as you work through this, and other, chapters, that you apply your reflection to the service user group with whom you are working, so that it immediately becomes relevant to your practice context.

Developing a relationship with the service user is critical to the success of the intervention. If the service user does not trust you, they are unlikely to engage with you, and unlikely to make the changes necessary to enhance their lives or safeguard themselves or others. As the chapter progresses you will be asked to reflect on the skills required to engage a service user effectively. Furthermore, understanding how the service user may be feeling when you begin working with them is a useful exercise that will enable you to develop your empathy for the service user.

Reflective Task 4.1

You have been on placement for three weeks and are asked to do your first visit to a service user.

How will you be feeling?

How might the service user be feeling?

It is likely that you will be feeling anxious or nervous, but imagine how the service user might be feeling because of your visit. It is important that you understand their feelings, and adjust your communication to meet their needs. Ingram et al. (2014) discuss the centrality to reflecting on your self, professional boundaries and your communication skills in the creation of working service-user relationships.

Social work is a holistic role that can only be achieved effectively by using a wide range of skills. Other chapters will discuss the importance of applying your knowledge of social work theory, agency policy and legislation, and reflection on your intervention skills and values, which will all support your ability to develop your relationship-building skills. Intervention skills should never be seen in isolation, but supported with robust reflection and application of knowledge.

Brannan et al (2018) remind us of a variety of ladders of participation, reflecting on the importance of how much you involve the service user in decision making about the service that they will receive. Originally created to engage citizens in community planning, the ladder of participation (Arnstein, 1969) is highly transferable to service user engagement for a social work student, and Brannan et al (2018) demonstrate how this ladder has been developed to do so by different authors. A student social worker should avoid *non-participation*, where the student social worker enforces a service onto a service user, and *tokenistic* service user involvement, where the service user is asked for their wishes and feelings, but they are not considered in decision making. Instead, Brannan et al (2018) argue, the service user should be empowered to participate in decisions about their own services, with an aim to take *control* of decision making. Services such as family group conferencing, which originated in New Zealand as an inclusive provision to hear Maori needs rather than impress Western values and responses upon families, demonstrate excellent models of service user control and participation.

As a student social worker, you cannot instigate a sudden change of policy so that you ensure service user control and independence. However, you can be minded to ensure *partnership* working at all times, whereby you seek the service user's wishes and feelings, ensure they are fully informed in all aspects of practice that relates to them, and that they are supported to make informed decisions and are participant in all decision-making forums. For example, explaining the meeting and process and seeking a child's wishes and feelings before a child protection conference that they do not wish to attend can still ensure that their voice is heard within the decision-making process.

Further to that, *empowering* a service user should always be a goal for a student social worker. The Chinese proverb 'give a man a fish he will eat today, teach a man to fish and you feed him for a lifetime' epitomises empowerment. If you give your service user the skills to make a decision, the confidence to do so, and support them to identify the positive outcomes of having done so, they will be more likely to be able to use the skills in the future. Not only does this shift the power, but it enhances service users' futures and reduces service re-referrals. Brannan et al (2018) reminds us that there are many forms of power that a student social worker holds and that a service user will inevitably feel powerless as they begin a working relationship. However, acknowledgement and harnessing of a service user's strengths, knowledge and motivation can lead to addressing power differentials as you will be working on a higher rung of the ladder of participation.

COMMUNICATION SKILLS

In order to engage a service user, you must develop your communication skills. Beesley et al. (2018) reflect that good communication skills come from the use of listening, clarification, empathy and challenging skills, whilst Healy (2018) offers excellent advice on how to communicate effectively with different service user groups. Beesley et al. argue that by listening, using verbal and non-verbal communication skills with the service user you can elicit their wishes and feelings and what they would like from your service, which you should clarify by summarising to ensure that you have not only listened but heard and correctly understood their perspective. You should also be empathic, using your ability to understand and express to a service user how they are feeling in a given situation, putting aside your perspective. Howe (2013) reflects that empathy engages a service user because they feel valued. Nevertheless, remember that as a student social worker you may also have to challenge the service user's perspective. This may be to support their own reflection on their needs, to help them to see things from a different perspective, or may be because agency procedure and/or service provision do not match their expectations.

▬▬▬ Top Tips to Cultivate your Relationship with a Service User ▬▬▬

1   *Be open and honest*: the service user will be able to tell when your verbal communication is incongruent with your non-verbal communication. They need to be able to trust you.

2   *Play communication ping pong*: communication is a two-way interaction; to keep the ball in play you will need to use open questions and responses to keep a conversation going.

3   *Time spent in preparation is time well used*: preparing for your intervention mentally and physically will enhance engagement.

4   *Actively listen*: ensure that you *hear* what is said without distraction or analysis.

5   *Be actively empathic*: ensure that you demonstrate to the other person that you have heard and understood their perspective.

6   *Don't be afraid to check details*: clarifying that you both have the same perception prevents misunderstanding and frustration.

7   *Challenge when appropriate*: develop a sensitivity for when to challenge and what is the most effective way to do so for you and the other person.

8   *Develop your emotional intelligence*: by developing your awareness of your own strengths and weaknesses, and an understanding of how a service user may be impacted by your presence, you will enhance your communication skills.

When working with different service users, it will be important to consider different intervention styles. You will naturally develop an intervention style that suits your own skills; for example, if you are an optimist then a strengths perspective approach is likely to be your preferred style. It will also be influenced by the predominant intervention style of both your training and your placement. For example, a student may have been influenced by a particularly stimulating lecture on motivational interviewing and feels that their personality suits this method of intervention. Once on placement, they may be influenced by an agency philosophy that restorative practice both values service users and effective. Their practice will be influenced by each of these factors and the student will begin to develop a positive style of intervention. Nevertheless, a flexible approach to different service users will be critical. Being able to use different intervention styles will be important to ensure that your practice remains service user focused. Hill et al. (2019) advocate understanding, and being able to practice, a range of interventions to best meet a service user's needs.

RELIABLE, RESPECTFUL AND RESOURCEFUL

When engaging service users, you will need to be *reliable*, *respectful* and *resourceful*. In order to be *reliable*, you will need to do what you said you would do. You will need to be organised to enable you to be where you said you would be at the agreed time, or to undertake the agreed task. It will be important that you only agree to undertake an achievable task, so always reflect upon viability before you commit to a role. If in doubt, be open and honest with your service user that you are unsure, but that you will clarify the information or procedure and come straight back to them (and make sure you do). If you are reliable, the service user will develop trust in you, which will enhance the working relationship and enable you to achieve greater outcomes with them. Ensure that you have explained your role, including what they can and cannot expect of you, so that they know the confines of your role. For example, issues of confidentiality where you cannot promise to keep a secret for them, as all information should be recorded within your agency system. By being open and honest you are also being reliable, as they will know your boundaries.

When working with a service user, you must be *respectful* of them. This comes in a number of different guises. First, and perhaps most obvious within social work, you must respect their individual background, including their culture, gender, age, faith and class. The very foundation of your social work values is based upon respecting every service user as an individual, and working to ensure that you seek *their* wishes and feelings to enable person-centred practice to be used effectively.

> We must consider each situation in its own right, rather than apply general principles in an oversimplified and dogmatic way. (Thompson, 2012: 5)

HCPC (2016) entrenches this in expected social work student practice throughout the guidance. Furthermore, Thompson's (1992) personal, cultural and structural (PCS) analysis theoretical model reminds us that service users will have experienced PCS oppression, and that as a social work student you will need to be aware of the oppression that they may have experienced and the impact it may have had on them and their ability to engage with you as a social work student, whilst not assuming their individualised experience. Thompson (2012) argues that a good social worker should be aware of potential oppression suffered, whilst considering, and indeed valuing, their diversity as a strength.

Hill et al. (2019) reflect on the need for cultural competence when working with a service user, which they remind us is a mix of cultural knowledge, awareness and sensitivity, citing Weaver (1999). Therefore a balance of understanding different cultural perspectives, yet not assuming the impact, is required. Tedam (2012) recommends the MANDELA model (Make, Acknowledge, Needs, Differences, Education, Life, Age), where the person's historical and cultural experiences are considered when working with them. Whilst she initially wrote this reflecting on practice educators understanding the learning needs of black-African heritage students, it is an excellent model to use when working with a service user who is of a different cultural background than your own. To enhance service user engagement, you should *make* time to listen to and *acknowledge* the service user's perspective and *needs*, whilst acknowledging the *differences* between self and service user, and ensure that you take account of their *educational* and *life* experiences when reflecting on their needs, and be aware of *age* differences when considering power differentials that impact on ability to be open and honest with you. Laird and Tedam (2019) state that we live and practice in a diverse society and that our practice has to reflect an understanding of the ethical dilemmas of working with a wide range of service users to enable us to become culturally competent social workers.

Reflective Task 4.2

When approaching a new service user, what different methods can you use to ensure that you understand their perspective?

Remember that your practice educator is a rich source of support and knowledge to enable you to reflect on such issues. Rankine et al. (2018) agree that reflective social work supervision enhances outcomes for service users, as the social worker is better placed to be able to understand the socially constructed oppression and social justice issues the service user experiences.

Respect also comes from using the previously discussed communication skills. If you listen accurately to the service user's wishes and feelings and convey what you have heard through clarification and empathy, you will have valued the service user's perspective and demonstrated respect. It will be easier for you to challenge different perspectives if you provide an evidence-based explanation that takes account of their perspective, as the service user will feel that whilst you may not agree with all their opinions and wishes, you have considered them.

Finally, you should work to become a *resourceful* social work student. Definitions of professionalism provide social work students with interesting dilemmas, as they are asked in equal measures to comply to agency policy and procedure, yet are required to be creative and person-centred. By advocating that you become a resourceful social work student, I do not encourage you to dismiss the agency procedure file. You will need to adhere to this to be able to demonstrate professionalism and capability within your assessed placement. However, a good social worker should be able to assess when it is appropriate to advocate strongly to a manager that this is the exception to the procedural rule, to draw on a wide repertoire of skills and strategies to engage a wide range of service users, and to think *outside the box* to resolve a problem.

Reflective Task 4.3

Jack, a five-year-old child, has poor school attendance because his mother misuses drugs and struggles to get organised in a morning. She always collects him promptly and meets many of his other emotional and physical needs.

How do you feel about collecting him each morning and dropping him at school?

This is an interesting dilemma. Many qualified social workers will tell you that this is not within the social work role, and that a mother is responsible for her child's welfare. They will argue that by creating a false dependency that it masks a greater problem. Nevertheless, other social workers will argue the reverse: that by undertake this simple task you enable the child to receive an education, and enhancing outcomes is a social workers role, that this a resourceful, preventative role. What do you think about each perspective? If the mother was ill rather than a drug misuser, would this change your perspective? Would you do it in the short term whilst other resolutions could be found by the mother? I would suggest that if you as a social work student can offer a resourceful solution, you should discuss this with your practice educator so that together you can gauge its appropriateness, and hopefully the practice educator will be able to enhance your creative solution with their expertise.

IMPACT OF SELF ON SERVICE USERS

Emotional intelligence is an importance aspect of being a social worker. In Chapter 1 we discussed understanding yourself, your strengths and areas for development to develop your emotional intelligence, and Chapter 7 reflects upon the need for emotional resilience in difficult situations. However, a further strand of your emotional intelligence is understanding the impact of your self on service users. Being able to reflect upon and begin to understand how you are perceived by service users will enable you to develop your skills in working with service users, and ultimately optimise service users' outcomes.

┌─────────────────────┐
│ **Reflective Task 4.4** │
└─────────────────────┘

How do you think you are seen by service users?

In answering this question, it may be difficult to put your self aside and see how you are perceived by others. First, consider how your normal style of communication and intervention impact on the service user, and adjust this dependent on the service user's individualised needs. Some service users will need a clear, direct response, whilst others will find that overwhelming and counter-productive. However, there will also be circumstances that you will need to consider how your participation impacts on the response of the service user. For example, if a service user reacts to your update angrily, do you consider that to be because of what you said, or do you reflect on *how* you said it? A service user's reaction is never isolated, it will be impacted by events in their own life, both immediate and historical, the content of the discussion, and your relationship and delivery. For instance, if you feel anxious or confident it may impact on your presentation and the service user will respond to you differently. Ingram (2015) reflects upon the impact of your emotions on your practice, and highlights that emotional intelligence enables the student social worker to be more empathic as you become aware of the impact of your self on the intervention.

Feedback from your practice educator (see Chapter 2) or from the service user (as will be discussed below) will enable this process through corroboration of your reflections and stimulation of new ideas. If you are open to hearing and reflecting upon and actioning the changes recommended in constructive feedback, you will be able to enhance your communication and intervention skills, thereby enhancing your social work practice.

GATHERING SERVICE USER FEEDBACK

Initial engagement with a service user will be critical to your successful working relationship. You will need to explain to them your student status. This will include that you will complete a port-folio, assignment and/or reflections that might include references to themselves, and explain your system of redaction to ensure their anonymity, as discussed in Chapter 8. By discussing with the service user at this early stage your student status and need for constructive feedback to help you to enhance your skills, you will be able to engage them in a meaningful feedback dialogue. By set-ting out your student status, you will also set out the time-limited boundaries that will naturally present themselves to your work with them, as you will cease working with them as your place-ment ceases, unless you are lucky enough to be offered a job within your placement team. And finally, by setting out your student status initially, you will counter a little of the power imbalance between yourself as the service provider and themselves as the service receiver. This understanding that you too can be vulnerable is an empowering experience for a service user. It is one that you can and should harness to utilise their understanding of how it feels to be a service user.

Fenge et al. (2014) quote Sadd (2011) who advocates service user participation in all elements of placement development as it is beneficial to both service user and student. Whilst you may not be able to control if a service user is invited to your PLA meeting or to meet you in induction week, you do have the control to facilitate the quality and quantity of service user involvement as your placement progresses. Discuss if you could arrange a time to meet with them to hear their experiences of being a service user, both positive and less positive. so that you can build your knowledge base of how service user experience service provision. Brannan et al. (2018) describe this a *personal narrative* and argue that it is a powerful learning opportunity. This will enhance both your practice and your academic work.

Fenge et al. (2014) also remind us that short-term work may not give you time to develop a working relationship that enables you to gather feedback. If you have a placement that works with service users for a short time only, work with your practice educator to plan a way to circumvent this. Perhaps in your initial (or indeed only) meeting with the service user, you could explain your student status and the value of meaningful feedback to your practice and request to undertake a follow-up visit or telephone call. Resourceful solutions may be required to facilitate this, but they are still worth undertaking.

Reflective Task 4.5

You are planning your first direct observation. How will you ensure that you include the service user in your preparation, observation and feedback?

Chapter 2 includes discussion on how to plan your direct observation, but here I ask you to think specifically from a service user's perspective. How will you ensure that they are truly able to make an informed decision about participation? Are you able to plan the content of the session with them, or does that skew the naturalness of the observation? How will you ensure that you gather meaningful feedback so that they can be open and honest with you without bias, and so that you can understand their perspective?

It is only through cultivating a positive relationship from the start of your placement that this will be viable. The importance of starting your placement with this positive, inclusive approach becomes clearer as you realise that everything stems from your working relationship with your service user. Time spent initially engaging a service user will be highly beneficial to your development and progress as you are able to engage them in meaningful learning experiences. Fenge et al. (2014) reflect that service user involvement is more often tokenistic than meaningful, and it is on meaningful feedback that we would like you to reflect. Pearl et al. (2018) argue that for service user feedback to be influential in developing the social work student it needs to be used as a reflective tool, for example to stimulate discussion in supervision. This will enable you to consider their perspective and incorporate into your practice development.

....

POTENTIAL PLACEMENT *PITFALL* Garry was doing well on placement. He was able to independently manage a range of practice learning opportunities and was effective at reflecting on his practice and applying theory. He and his practice educator were confident that he was successfully on track to pass placement. As part of his portfolio, Garry was required to gather a minimum of two pieces of service user feedback, and he did just that. He asked two of his best service users to complete a simple yes/no questionnaire about if they had found him reliable, respectful and resourceful. They both answered 'yes' to all his questions, and he duly put them into his portfolio and immediately forgot them as they were unable to evidence any capabilities: Garry had developed despite the service user feedback.

POTENTIAL PLACEMENT *OPPORTUNITY* Henry was doing well on placement. He was able to independently manage a range of practice learning opportunities and was effective at reflecting on his practice and applying theory. He and his practice educator were confident that he was successfully on track to pass placement. As part of his portfolio, Henry was required to gather a minimum of two pieces of service user feedback. He asked his service users early in placement if he would be able to meet with each of them and his practice educator towards the end of placement. He had built a good rapport by asking for feedback on a regular basis and the service user had been able to see that he had applied his feedback to enhance his practice. The practice educator was able to evidence a strong working partnership that was based on mutual trust and respect as the service user was able to provide both positive and constructive feedback on how he could enhance his practice. Henry was able to use the minutes of the meetings to robustly evidence a range of capabilities. Henry had developed exponentially because of the service user feedback.

....

Whilst the second option may take longer to achieve, as a student you have the luxury of time. If you can achieve a positive learning experience for yourself, the service user and the practice educator, you will all be richer, and you will be a much better social worker. Speers and Lathlean's (2015) research identified that it benefitted service users to be empowered to provide feedback to students (as the research was situated in a mental health service, recovery was cited as enhanced by this involvement). They identified that social work students sometimes were reluctant to gather service user feedback, but that once done some students even felt that service user feedback had more impact than their practice educator's feedback – so do not be afraid to gather it. Of course, you must be open to receiving feedback, as Chapters 3 and 7 discuss in relation to practice educator feedback.

Nevertheless, do not dismiss a written questionnaire out of hand, just ensure that you plan the questions to enable constructive feedback to be provided. Or think resourcefully using a word association game or drawing task for children. Concerns will always be raised that the feedback you gather can never be truly objective, as you will inevitably have a working relationship with the service user that impacts upon it, and power dynamics may restrict the service user's desire to be truly open and honest. As a student you should always ask your practice educator to supplement your feedback with the feedback that they seek. This is not about them talking about you behind your back, but a further opportunity to enhance your practice through reliable and constructive feedback. Hughes (2017) studied qualified social workers' reflections on the longer-term impact of service user involvement in their social work education and found that the benefits included valuing the service user's experiences, views and perspective as critical to successful intervention outcomes, and the positive impact of constructive feedback on their practice development.

■■■■■■ PLACEMENT PERSPECTIVE 4.2 ■■■■■■

Student perspective on engaging service users

I found that honesty, reliability and empathy are skills that really help with engaging service users. Service user feedback highlighted that I had positive working relationships and that I work with the service user from my heart not because I should, which showed that I valued them.

I learnt how important my emotional wellbeing was. In order to be of any help to a service user, I needed to be emotionally stable, and I would always put my problems to one side when I met the service user. By understanding my role as enabler rather than rescuer, I could appreciate the positive changes I saw through helping service users to change their own lives.

I can see how my relationships with the service users developed through my placement, particularly professional boundaries. I inadvertently shared too much information with the service users, consequently they saw me as a friend and would try and contact me outside office hours. I was able to reflect on my mistakes, and by establishing clear boundaries with the service users at the first meeting, it helped alleviate confusion over the purpose of our working relationship. I learnt to maintain my personality whilst keeping information about myself limited and relevant.

Freya Svendsen, BA Social Work Student

CHAPTER SUMMARY

This chapter has asked you to reflect on the benefits of involving your service users in your development. First, you are asked to consider your communication skill development and the positive impact that will have on demonstrating capability in your intervention skills. Consideration is given to the issues you may need to think about to ensure that you can engage the service user, including being reliable, respectful and resourceful. Then attention is turned to the inclusion of service users in feedback provision and how it can enhance your practice to hear the service user perspective on your practice.

CHAPTER CHECKLIST

✔ Develop good communication skills to engage service users and enable you to demonstrate intervention skills.
✔ Involve service users in decision making wherever possible, and take account of their wishes and feelings when it is not.

✔   Develop your emotional intelligence to enable you to engage the service user.
✔   Be reliable, respectful and resourceful.
✔   Gather service user feedback throughout the placement to build skills and confidence.

■■■■■■■■■■ **Further reading** ■■■■■■■■■■

Beesley, P., Watts, M. and Harrison, M. (2018) *Developing Your Communication Skills in Social Work*. London: SAGE.

Chapter 7 'Meaningful service user and carer involvement in student placements', in Fenge, L., Howe, K., Hughes, M. and Thomas, G. (2014) *The Social Work Portfolio: A Student's Guide to Evidencing your Practice*. Maidenhead: Open University Press.

Healy, K. (2018) *The Skilled Communicator in Social Work: The Art and Science of Communication in Practice*. London: Palgrave.

Hill, D., Agu, L. and Mercer, D. (2019) *Exploring and Locating Social Work*. London: Red Globe.

Chapter 16 'The voice of service users and carers', in Lishman, J., Yuill, C., Brannan, J. and Gibson, A. (eds) (2018) *Social Work: An Introduction*. London: SAGE.

5

UNDERSTANDING YOUR SOCIAL WORK SKILLS, KNOWLEDGE AND VALUES IN YOUR PROFESSIONAL PRACTICE

This chapter will provide discussion on the need for the social work student to develop understanding of a breadth of skills, including professionalism, the ability to apply theory to practice and the skill of understanding their own and other's values, discussing often complex ethical dilemmas. The student will be asked to reflect throughout on their own skill development and the holistic nature of being a social worker.

PLACEMENT PERSPECTIVE 5.1

Practice educator's perspective on a student demonstrating holistic capability within placement

When assessing development for a student, I need to see a willingness to learn from new experiences and evidence of how their renewed understanding and skills develop over the course of the placement. I expect a student to review and increasingly recognise their own strengths and areas that they need to focus on. This requires ongoing reflection and application of theory to their practice. Over the course of the placement students should demonstrate a broader and more eclectic skill base, evidencing how they may have adapted or developed their approach based on reflection and/or changing circumstances.

I am keen to see an emerging professional identity, by making use of learning opportunities to explore different approaches and styles and be able to articulate what personal and professional values or principles this draws from. I find it invaluable for the social work student to ensure that they refer to how this links with their accountability as a professional, referencing social work principles and codes of practice as well as providing evidence of a growing understanding of self both in how they manage the emotional impact of the work and their ability to articulate the complex nature and ethical

(Continued)

dilemmas in situations they face when balancing rights and risks, care and control.

Within supervision and placement, I value a willingness to enquire and question, including my own perspective and practice. A student who demonstrates that they remain curious and are prepared to challenge, taking the initiative to understand the roles of other agencies and asking why and how procedures and ways of working are established within this area of social work is a strong student. They need to understand diversity, how groups are marginalised and oppressed by societal structures as well as individuals. They should recognise the strength of identity and culture and evidence the opportunities and limitations of their role as social worker when seeking to empower service users.

In order to holistically pass placement a student needs to demonstrate a commitment to reading and research to evidence an increasingly wider knowledge base in regard to the service users they are working with and are able to refer to up-to-date knowledge in supervision, evidencing awareness of relevant current affairs and media attitudes as well as social work articles and journals. However, it is not enough just to know, students need to *apply*. They need to take the opportunity to explore how and why they might have acted, not just assume it was an automatic response. They need to refer to the specific topics covered in the course modules and make connections with practice. They should reflect upon the knowledge they draw on to understand the person, the circumstances and in turn how they frame their interventions. The student also needs to evidence how they have followed the relevant law, policies and procedures used within the placement and presenting how and why this is appropriate.

Gail Barlow, Off-Site Practice Educator

HOLISTIC CAPABILITY

As a student contemplating a career in social work, it is likely that you thought you would be good at social work because you are caring and compassionate and want to 'do' things to help people within society. Hopefully, as you have worked through this book you will have begun to identify that being on placement is so much more than being good with people. You will need to work within legislative boundaries and agency procedures and also have an understanding of how social work theory impacts upon and informs your practice as well as an understanding of your personal and professional values to guide your decision making to enable you to act professionally, which requires reflecting on your practice to ensure that you are always developing your practice to the best of your ability. You will need to demonstrate a holistic capability that encompasses all of these skills.

POTENTIAL PLACEMENT *PITFALL* Fiona was excellent at engaging service users. Service users provided feedback that she was valued because she spent considerable time each week with them, and they felt cared for, she would 'do everything for me'.

However, she was not working with agency guidelines, nor was she able to identify the social work theory that she was using. She was very happy that she was being praised and found it difficult to hear that she needed to empower, not enable, her service users towards independence.

POTENTIAL PLACEMENT *OPPORTUNITY* Gill was excellent at engaging service users. Service users provided feedback that she was valued because she spent considerable time each week with them, and they felt cared for, she would 'do everything for me'.

However, she reflected on this feedback and began to wonder if she was doing her service users a disservice as she was not empowering them to be independent, and wondered how they would cope when her placement ended and she was no longer available. She discussed her thoughts with her practice educator. She spoke to them about their wishes and feelings and began to identify alternative areas of support that would empower them. She wrote a reflection on her practice and the theory that she had identified.

You need to develop your skills in all areas, don't ignore one for the other as they are all equally important. Your practice educator's role is to support you in the development of all of these areas, so access their support throughout placement to augment your learning.

Reflective Task 5.1

When you cross a road what skills do you draw on?

It is likely that you will use both your sight and sound senses to assess the safety when crossing the road. But you will also draw on your knowledge of road safety and learning from previous experiences both positive and negative, yet be making decisions based on that particular road crossing. You may be aware of other people, perhaps watch when they feel it is safe to cross, or may be influenced by individualised circumstances like a need to get to a shop before it closes. Even simple decision-making situations are influenced by a variety of factors. Social work is no different; every intervention, meeting or discussion will be influenced by a variety of issues.

Reflective Task 5.1 (continued)

When you last undertook a home visit to a service user, what skills, knowledge and values did you draw on to ensure that you were professional?

You will have created a unique list, as you are an individual and the intervention will raise distinctive issues dependent on its content. As you read through this chapter, consider this reflective task and identify your strengths and areas to develop in each section.

PROFESSIONALISM

Social work is a profession: one cannot be a social worker without a social work qualification. That is right and proper, you will look after the most vulnerable people in society. Beckett et al. (2017) argue that the profession of social work is different from many other professions as often the service user is reluctant to engage. Additionally, they may be at a stage in their life where they are most in need, but find it hardest to access support. As a social worker you are expected to abide by a set of professional rules. BASW (2014) set out a code of ethics to follow, and although Social Work England took responsibility for such issues from March 2019, the HCPC (2017a) *Guidance on Conduct and Ethics for Students* sets out clear expectations in relation to a student social worker's behaviour and professionalism. Banks (2016) argues that professionalism requires a commitment to and critical reflexivity of these ethics and requirements. Discussion with your practice educator enables you to explore why each element of professionalism and challenging of existing assumptions will enhance your understanding of how you can demonstrate professionalism.

Beckett et al. (2017: 74) argue that social work students demonstrate professionalism by a 'certain way of conducting themselves', and go on to discuss competence in and commitment to social work tasks as indicators. In Chapter 4 I asked you to reflect on the importance of being *reliable*, *respectful* and *resourceful*, which all contribute to a professional approach. Good time-keeping and organisational skills value and respect service users as it suggests to the service user that you feel they are worth making the effort for. Listening to the service user and providing a person-centred approach that takes account of their individual experiences, strengths and needs also demonstrates a dedication to social work professional values. Whilst creative solutions to problems show a commitment that also underpins the notion of professionalism.

However, accountability is also absolutely fundamental to professional social work. Laming (2003) made it abundantly clear that no social worker should make decisions alone, and that case management supervision is a critical element in safeguarding against risk. As a student social worker, one of the first points you should learn is to discuss with your practice educator (and then as a qualified social worker, your manager) all your practice learning opportunities so that they have oversight of your work. That is not to say that you should not be able to make decisions independently, as a further element of professionalism is the ability to use your initiative in response to service users' needs. A good social work student is able to present a formulated plan to their practice educator for their approval.

....

PROSPECTIVE PLACEMENT *PITFALL* Natasha arrived at the interprofessional meeting late, making excuses that made it clear that she accepted no responsibility for her own actions. Within the meeting she was unable to present pertinent information because she had not prepared her thoughts on the risks to the service user, who afterwards was dismissive of Natasha as he felt unsupported and let-down by her behaviour in the meeting. Key risk factors were not raised, as new information was not shared and no support plan was formulated.

In her next supervision, Natasha's practice educator raised concerns that she had received complaints about her conduct in a meeting, of which the practice educator had not been aware that she was attending.

POTENTIAL PLACEMENT *OPPORTUNITY* Lucy knew that the interprofessional meeting would be difficult: she had to raise identified risks yet advocate for the service user's rights. First, she sought support from her practice educator and together they planned how Lucy would prepare for the meeting to enable her to be confident and assertive within the meeting. Before the meeting Lucy spent time writing a summary of the risks that the service user faced and their strengths. She was clear what service provision her agency could provide, and the areas she hoped other services could. She visited the service user before the meeting and spent time preparing him for it.

Lucy arrived at the meeting early and quickly reviewed with her practice educator her goals. Within the meeting, she was able to present her report clearly, despite feeling very nervous. Her practice educator had put the meeting in her diary to be there for moral support, and was able to prompt Lucy when a small but relevant piece of information was overlooked.

In the next supervision, Lucy received praise from her practice educator and positive feedback from the chair of the meeting.

....

.... **Reflective Task 5.2** ....

Which social work student represents the professionalism of social work?

Where would you consider your professionalism in relation to attending such a meeting?

....

Professionalism is demonstrated through strong skills in an intervention that are underpinned by their knowledge and value base. Banks (2016) argues that professional integrity is a key way to demonstrate one's values and respect the service user. Professionalism can be seen to be a commitment to ongoing development, a critically reflective approach to your self, and a proactive involvement in reflective supervision. It becomes abundantly clear that professionalism is essential to enable you to practice effectively, but that professionalism is a holistic skill that brings in all the other skills talked about throughout this book.

VALUES

Professionalism is critical because it values the service user and demonstrates a commitment to enhancing their lives.

> [I]n resolving social work *who we are* is as important as *what we do*. (Carter and Hugman, 2014: 1)

When using statutory powers, professionalism ensures fairer service provision for service users, who may have experienced multiple oppressive incidents. A professional approach to treat the service user as an individual worthy of respects values them and is a step towards restoring self-esteem.

Beckett et al. (2017: 4) argue that 'our values are the basis on which we act'. They go on reflect that different groups of society have different values that are shaped by the group's cultural and social identity. You will have explored in your course what are social work values, but you will also hold personal values based on your gender, faith, ethnicity, class and age. How you view an issue will influence how you respond to it, so an understanding of how you view the world is important in your social work development. It is difficult to separate the two. A better response is to reflect upon how they influence you.

....

POTENTIAL PLACEMENT *PITFALL* Niamh's personal values were based on her faith-based perspective, where she believed that same-sex relationships were not appropriate. When asked to work with a same-sex couple, she did so, believing that she could separate personal and professional values. In supervision discussion, the practice educator raised concerns that Niamh had made recommendations that were subconsciously based on her personal values. Niamh was not open to exploring this idea as she felt that she could separate her roles, and concerns were inevitably raised about her ability to be non-judgemental in meeting the service user's needs.

POTENTIAL PLACEMENT *OPPORTUNITY* Erin's personal values were based on her faith-based perspective, where she believed that same-sex couples were not appropriate. When asked to work with a same-sex couple, she asked to discuss her personal values in supervision. She and her practice educator were able to explore the basis for her values, both from a social work perspective as well as a faith perspective, which enabled her to explore and adapt her values to a more inclusive stance. After the work was completed, she was able to reflect on her assumptions and experience working with the couple, and identified clear learning that she was able to use as evidence for her value development.

....

This is not to say that you should wholeheartedly reject the values with which you grew up, but that as a social work student you are expected to reflect on the impact of your personal values upon your professional practice. In order to develop your professional values, you need to be aware of internalised stereotypes and assumptions that you make without thinking about it. For example, if you visit a single mum you will react differently from the way you will react to a visit to a single dad – you have been socially conditioned to consider that women care and work, whilst men work. Exploration in supervision and reflections will enhance your ability to recognise your own assumptions and take actions to minimise the effect that they have on your service provision. Papouli (2014: 233) reflects that it is the discussion in supervision of the application of values to the social work student's practice that enables the student to explore their values, and advocates the benefit of the practice educator as a *positive ethical role model*.

Reflective discussion will be critical to develop your social work values. Carter and Hugman (2014) discuss the fluidity of values. As part of your ongoing development, you must review and evaluate your values regularly. As a social work student, you are likely to quickly encounter ethical dilemmas that challenge your social work assumptions. Beckett et al. (2017) reflect on conflict within your professional values and acknowledge that it is rarely simple.

Consider which is more important to you: a service user's right to self-determination, or a service user's needs to be met?

Both are important, but sometimes we will face a situation where we cannot do both. This raises an ethical dilemma where you have to consider the impact of choosing one value above another. Discussion in supervision will support your exploration of your thoughts on this. Bell (2018) recognises that an ethical dilemma may result in a mix of positive and negative outcomes, but that by reflective discussion the best outcome for that time, situation and service user is sought. He recognises the wisdom of seeking others' views to validate or challenge and develop your own.

This chapter does not seek to explore each minority area, but instead considers the importance of an individual approach that takes account of the service user's and your own social, cultural and life similarities and differences and the impact on service provision, as discussed in Chapter 4. Beckett et al. (2017) reflect on diversity amongst service users, and acknowledge that it can be hard to assess the needs of someone with whom you do not identify. The need for good communication skills is never more relevant than in such a situation. As a social work student, you need to recognise and understand a service user's cultural, social and life experience, again discussed in Chapter 4, whilst not making assumptions based on those factors. Listening to the service user's unique experiences of their own life is critical to enable you to value the service user in a person-centred way. In Placement Perspective 4.1, Myrtle Oke requests as a service user that you treat her as an individual, whilst understanding her shared experiences of oppression. Hill et al. (2019) advocate a cultural competence through understanding of the shared experiences, oppression and triumphs of a group, but also recognise that this both changes over time and is different for sub-groups within a culture (e.g. different age groups will experience their cultural roots differently). They advocate a critical approach to diversity, asking you to reflect, as Myrtle does, on the service user's individual circumstances by listening to their perspective, but base it within a position of knowledge through cultural competence.

Thompson's (1992) PCS model of analysis provides an excellent framework for understanding the layers of oppression that a service user may have encountered before entering your service provision, and Tedam's (2012) MANDELA model reminds us to take account of their cultural and social history. Many of our service users have experienced oppression and discrimination, and a significant role of the social worker is to empower the service user to achieve their full potential and fight social injustice to enhance the service user's rights.

On a practical note, your professionalism and values come together when issues of confidentiality arise. As a social work student, you are expected to share all information about your service user within your placement agency in the form of written recordings or case notes, and to discuss developments in relation to your practice learning opportunities with your practice educator, and sometimes manager. However, time spent reflecting on the ethical merits of this will develop your values. How do you ensure that the service user knows the recording procedure, and who has access to such information? Beesley et al. (2018) discuss that information sharing outside your placement agency (i.e. with other relevant professionals) should only be undertaken with the service user's knowledge and within agency procedures.

Reflective Task 5.4

A service user asks you if she can share something with you 'in total confidence'. What do you do?

Confidentiality is so important, as it values the service user and demonstrates professionalism. However, in such a case you should not put yourself in a position of having 'to keep a secret'. If a service user asked this, you should always be clear that that was not possible. As a student social worker, you should never be in a position where you have information that you are unable to share with your practice educator or placement. When you start working with a service user, you will need to set out the limitations of confidentiality, that as a representative of the agency, information shared will be documented within agency documents, but that non-relevant personnel will not have access to it, and that it will not be shared outside the agency without their permission unless it is to protect and safeguard the service user or others. In order to continue to respect and value a service user if they place themselves or others at risk, you should still only share that information with relevant people and inform the service user of your actions.

Breaches of confidentiality can result in concerns being raised on placement, or even placement termination. You have a duty to safeguard service user information, so leaving confidential files in your car whilst you pay for petrol on the way to court is not acceptable, so you must plan ahead to avoid this situation. You should not take service user information outside the office, so think about how you record service user names and addresses in a diary but are still able to access information on where to go. Chapter 8 explores the issues of confidentiality within your academic work. But a simple rule of thumb is that you should remove all identifiable information before it leaves the office to protect the service user.

Hill et al. (2019) remind us of the need to reflect on the power that comes with the role of social worker. They argue, based on Foucault (1979), that in order to be professional, you need to understand the knowledge base that you are working within, but that that knowledge base itself is intrinsically value-laden and powerful.

Reflective Task 5.5

As a social work student, reflect on how you felt starting in a new profession or even a new placement, and your confusion at the new 'language' of social work.

It is likely that you felt powerless due to your lack of understanding. Now transfer that feeling to a service user who is surrounded by that language, with decisions being made within a framework that they do not understand the rules, and by people who are often once removed from you as the face of the agency. How might the service user feel? What can you do to decrease that power imbalance?

You may feel powerless as a social work student, but to the service user, you are the powerful agent for the service. Your recommendations will determine whether they get a service, so a service user might feel unable to challenge you, or to be open and honest with you. Hill et al. (2019) remind us of the efficacy of the exchange model of assessment (Smale et al., 1993) in ensuring that the service user is participant in their own assessment and care planning. Remembering to be empathic about their previous experiences and anxiety facing their current situation, listening to their perspective and giving reliable information and support will begin to address the power imbalance, but it cannot be eradicated. A reflection of the impact of yourself as an agent of control is an excellent way to develop your understanding of your values.

KNOWLEDGE

Beckett and Horner (2016) argue that social workers have significant powers and responsibilities so have a duty to make *informed* decisions about people's lives. Indeed, this is a way to value service users by ensuring our professionalism and ability. It is based on knowledge and understanding of social work theories found in core textbooks and journals, which inform us why a service user might be acting in the way that they are (often referred to as a 'theory') and how different interventions (often referred to as 'models') might be beneficial to their outcomes. Furthermore, it is also based on understanding how a social policy impacts upon service provision, the legislative and procedural basis for your interventions, and how service provision works between a range of service and professions. It is important to read widely and critically; consider why a newspaper article is written from that perspective or how a research-based journal article informs your practice. Whilst always using the module reading list as a base to work from is essential, exploring other books and websites with a critical eye will enhance your understanding of the subject. Watching TED talks can be beneficial, as can engaging in organised webinars to reflect on the application of theory.

Beckett and Horner (2016) argue that social workers often use an eclectic mix of different social work theories when undertaking an intervention, as service users are commonly complex with multiple issues that call for flexible, creative, multifaceted responses. Indeed, Dunk-West (2018) reminds us that the complexity of working with service users means that social work research findings can never be 'one size fits all', as research is subjective and the service user's complex needs and history impact uniquely upon them. That is not to dismiss the importance of social work theory, and indeed as a social work student it is best to understand each one individually before you begin to amalgamate them. Reflective discussion in supervision enables the application of theory to practice, which is often when you are able to understand its nuances more than on initial presentation in a lecture. As discussed in Chapter 4, all work with a service user must come from a person-centred perspective, so when making an informed decision you should be considering the most appropriate knowledge to apply to that individual situation. Whilst Figure 5.1 does not cover every social work theory, it provides examples of those that might influence your intervention with a service user.

Figure 5.1   Key social work theories for intervention

Whilst the application of theory to practice should be undertaken within reflections and assignments, the development of it can be aided by your practice educator. Collingwood (2005) offers a structure to support reflection on applying theory to practice in social work student supervision. Her three-stage theory framework asks the student to first build a profile of the service user, including service provision history and personal details. Second, Collingwood (p. 9) asks that the theory is considered by student and practice educator and added in two parts: the 'theory to inform', which are theories such as sociological and psychological models that support the student to understand the service user; and the 'theory to intervene', which enables the student to consider the most appropriate intervention based on the service user's needs. Third, after the intervention Collingwood asks the student to consider which knowledge, skills and values they drew upon as they reflect on their practice in supervision with the practice educator. Her research identified that using this supervision strategy enhanced the reflective use of theory in supervision and increased the confidence of both social work student and practice educator.

Before undertaking an intervention:

Describe the service user's history and personal profile.

What theory/theories help you to understand the service user's needs?

What theory and model of intervention would enable you meet the service user's needs?

After undertaking the intervention, reflect upon:

Which skills did you use?

Which knowledge did you use?

Which personal and professional values did you draw upon?

Collingwood (2005) provides visual representation of the model to aid reflection on A3 paper, which makes it accessible for visual learners (see Chapter 1, VARK; Fleming and Mills, 1992). Theory absolutely implies reading textbooks and journal articles, but exploration of visual aids, such as theory cards, should never be discounted as a starting point to stimulate your understanding.

Finally, Hill et al. (2019) reflect that the current, and very positive, trend is for empowering social work interventions such as restorative practice, strengths-based practice and solution-focused interventions, that each build on identifying strengths and building the service user's confidence and abilities. They value the service user and put them at the centre of your practice, which is also a professional approach.

■ PLACEMENT PERSPECTIVE 5.2 ■

Student's perspective on developing their knowledge, professionalism and values on social work placement

When on placement it is important to consider which theories may be used for the specific service user group, and read about them from the beginning of placement. During supervision discussions I was able to recognise times I had used my knowledge to inform my practice and was supported to identify which theories may be useful to consider in future situations.

Skills can be demonstrated through working directly with service users, colleagues and other professionals. Feedback from formal

(Continued)

and informal observation is essential as this can be used to contribute towards reflection. I found that supervision and peer discussions contributed to me being able to identify and evidence my progression in line with the PCF.

A good degree of reflexivity in relation to one's own feelings and actions is also important. I feel that my time on placement allowed me to develop my personal and professional social work values. I used supervision and reflection to recognise when I had applied social work values to each scenario I was faced with, also being mindful of my personal values and how these can both impact on practice.

Siobhan Appleyard, BA Social Work Student

CHAPTER SUMMARY

Social work is a complex profession that requires understanding and development of a range of abilities to enable proficient support of the most vulnerable people in society. As a social work student, you are expected to develop holistically so that not only can you intervene effectively but that you also understand why from an evidence-based knowledge foundation and a professional value base. Your ability to practice professionally will underpin all your work and enable you to demonstrate capability as a student social worker. Your social work placement will offer collaborative support to enable that development. Your practical learning should be enhanced through time spent in informal and formal supervision discussing procedures and processes, values and application of knowledge to support your understanding of social work. Inevitably, developing your professionalism, knowledge base and values through reflection and collaborative supportive work with your practice educator will enhance your social work skills, and enable you to develop your working relationship with service users and professionals.

CHAPTER CHECKLIST

In order to maximise your holistic development on your social work placement:

✔ layer your learning by ensuring that you apply knowledge to your practice, reflect on your work, and consider your value base to ensure professionalism
✔ demonstrate professionalism by being organised, using your initiative and yet remaining accountable, and adhering to agency expectations
✔ explore your personal and professional values and be open to challenge yourself and your value base
✔ develop your knowledge of social work theories, models, legislation, social policy and procedures by discussion in supervision and application in reflections and assignments.

Further reading

Beckett, C. and Horner, N. (2016) *Essential Theory for Social Workers*. London: SAGE.

Health and Care Professions Council (HCPC) (2017a) *Guidance on Conduct and Ethics for Students*. London: HCPC.

Hill, D., Agu, L. and Mercer, D. (2019) *Exploring and Locating Social Work*. London: Red Globe.

Hugman, R. and Carter, J. (eds) (2016) *Rethinking Values and Ethics in Social Work*. London: Palgrave.

6

ENHANCING YOUR ABILITY TO CRITICALLY REFLECT

This chapter will concentrate on guidance and support on enhancing your ability to reflect. Consideration will be given as to why and how to undertake critically reflective writing, including exploration of different reflection models. The chapter will also explore verbal reflection in supervision and informal discussion, and personal ongoing reflection. As with previous chapters, there will be a discussion on collaborative learning with your practice educator.

PLACEMENT PERSPECTIVE 6.1

Practice educator's perspective on the importance of reflecting on social work placement

Reflection is the most beneficial skill that you will develop as a social work student. It underpins everything that you do in practice from assessment, planning, intervention through to review. It can be a daunting task that requires you to be open to self-critique and evaluation of feedback, but do not let that hold you back. In the same way that you observe practice to develop your own style, listen when colleagues are talking to each other about cases, as these informal chats are examples of verbal reflection.

Make use of your formal and informal supervisions as they are invaluable opportunities to explore your thinking and can provide a grounding for your written reflection. Your practice educator is there to help you explore your observations, views, assumptions, theoretical knowledge and values. I would suggest that good verbal reflection includes naming your feelings, recognising your own strengths and limitations, discussing applicable theory, an ability to negotiate differing opinions and coming to your own conclusions. Remember that this is a discussion so it allows for you to weigh up different perspectives and question all of your thinking. Be prepared for your practice educator to ask some questions that you may not have thought of to spark something new.

(Continued)

The more open you are with your feelings, the better your reflections can be because if you are not invested in the reflection you will not be invested in the learning that comes from it. Brush up on your feelings vocabulary to have the words to describe how you are feeling before starting placement so that you are prepared. Be honest with your practice educator about how you feel about reflection, whether you enjoy it, hate it or are confused about how it all works; they are there to guide you through it and teach you how to do it.

In contrast, written reflection should be focused, concise, clear and structured. Make use of reflection frameworks, which will give you a good base to reduce the volume of description, providing an evidence base whilst recognising the influence of your personal, professional and service values. Do not fall down a Google rabbit-hole of searching for research that matches what you are trying to say, simply use the knowledge and learning that you have been provided from university. Capturing your ability to be concise in a description of the event is crucial and supports your process of filtering relevant and critical information from the situation which you will use when completing assessments for service users.

Whether it be verbal or written, good reflection supports your professional development. Reflections can demonstrate your learning from difficult situations and celebrate your successes to understand what it was that you did well so that you continue doing it.

Fiona Adams, Practice Educator

WHY REFLECT?

A simplistic response to this is 'Because my university says that I have to', but being a social work student is so much more than that. Reflection should become a task that is deep-rooted in your being. Whitaker and Reimer (2017) found that often reflections were written to demonstrate competency rather than to enhance social work students' critical reflection on their practice development, and advocated that in order to learn the student must embrace an open and honest approach to writing reflections, free of anxiety about practice educator judgements. Throughout this book you have been asked to reflect. In Chapter 1 you were asked to reflect on your pre-placement self; in Chapters 3 and 4 your relationship with your practice educator and service users; and in Chapter 5 your values, skills and knowledge. Gardner (2014) argues that critical reflection is a holistic task, one that requires the reflector to consider how both the reflector and those around them are influenced. Reflection gives you understanding of the 'what', 'why' and 'how' of your social work interventions.

Reflective Task 6.1

Do you value reflection?

In Chapter 1, I asked you to consider your learning style (Honey and Mumford, 1986), and it may be that you are a reflector, in which case you will engage easily with this chapter and may not even need it. However, if you identified that reflection is not your learning style, particularly if you are an activist or pragmatist, you will benefit from reading this next section and reviewing your response to Reflective Task 6.1. Take time to understand why reflection is important, as until you embrace reflection, it will restrict your development on placement. Higgins (2019: 21) recognises that reflection can be hard at first, but becomes second nature the more you practice it, so that you might need reflective space, where you feel comfortable and are free to reflect uninterrupted.

> Reflective practice and the use of supervision … are a means of assisting social workers to understand the complexity and effectiveness of what is involved in the important task of social work. (Ingram et al., 2014: 84)

In recent years, every social work report has reinforced the need for reflective practice. Croisdale-Appleby's (2014: 82) review of social work education in England states that 'social workers require intellectual and emotional intelligence as well as self-awareness, self-confidence and self-reflection', whilst Munro (2017: 7) summarises that social workers must move away 'from a compliance culture to a learning culture', and recommends that knowledge, skills and reflection are the foundation of a capable workforce. As a result, reflection is embedded in the assessment criteria for social work students in the professional capability framework (PCF) (BASW, 2018) and guidance for qualified social workers in knowledge and skills statements (KSS) for both childrens (DfE, 2018) and adults (DoH, 2015) social workers.

When starting placement you will complete an induction period, as discussed in Chapter 3, where you will observe and reflect on practice and engage in reflective discussion in supervision on your initial impressions. Arguably, Dewey (1859–1952) was the godfather of modern experiential learning. He proposed, and others have developed his ideas, that by undertaking a task and reflecting on your successful and less-successful tasks to identify where you could enhance your practice, that you could try again with a better outcome. Sennett (2008) argues that experiential learning is maximised when a student receives *expressive instruction*, which he considers a combination of shadowing the practice educator to stimulate reflection on the student's preferred method of practice (modelling) combined with reflective discussion to enable the student to understand why it is done in that way and how it could be enhanced. Furthermore, Scragg (2019) argues that a practice educator's role is to ask challenging questions, not designed to trip you, but to stimulate reflection and develop your understanding. He goes on to suggest that the practice educator may not have all the answers, and that through reflective discussion you will both develop.

....

POTENTIAL PLACEMENT *PITFALL* James observed an assessment by a social worker and copied it exactly when he undertook his first assessment with a service user. He was surprised to find that his practice educator asked him to think about being more flexible in his approach.

(Continued)

POTENTIAL PLACEMENT *OPPORTUNITY* Lily observed an assessment by a number of different social workers. She was surprised to find that each one undertook it differently, so raised this in supervision. She and her practice educator discussed different techniques and she reflected on the needs of the individual service user, her own style of intervention and to embrace different elements of the observed assessments.

Social work placement is clearly an experiential learning opportunity where you undertake often complex tasks on a daily basis, then reflect on the tasks to identify, understand and own the change required. This requires reflection on layers of issues. The first is to enhance your emotional intelligence so that you can understand the impact that your intervention has on the service user and yourself, and make an informed decision to adjust your intervention style to maximise outcomes. Ferguson (2018) argues that at times the impact of the emotional toil on yourself can leave you unable to reflect *in action* (referring to Schon, 1983), so it can be seen that reflection *on action* will be critical to understanding how the stress of an intervention impacts on your ability to assess and adjust your responses. The second issue is to enhance your understanding of service users so that you can assess them more effectively, which will lead to more person-centred and appropriate interventions. Gardner (2014) argues that critical reflection requires an understanding of how issues impact upon the situation, for example cultural competence and the social construction of the service user's circumstances or understanding of the source of your values. For the third issue, Knott (2013: 11) coined the phrase 'informed reflective practioner' to describe the social worker who uses evidence-based reflection to enhance their understanding of a situation. It is clear that an understanding of how theory, social policy and legislation is applied to your practice will enhance your understanding of your intervention.

Hart (2018) recognises that reflective skills take time to develop, and only do so through regular practice. Bassot (2016) raises a word of caution that however good your reflective cycle may be, sometimes you may not evidence change, or even that your skills may regress. She argues, citing Illeris (2014), that this may be because you are asked to do too much too soon and feel overwhelmed with the learning task, or that whilst you recognise the need to change you are not yet ready to make that change. In either circumstance, discussion with your practice educator to find a solution will support your development.

Supervision and reflection are established staples of social work experiential learning. Ferguson (2018) argues, citing Casement (1985), that reflection is *internal supervision*. If supervision is like a tutorial to support you to develop your understanding of your intervention through application of knowledge and values to your skills, then reflection is self-directed study. Both are critical to your success as a developing social work student, and for your ongoing career.

WHAT IS REFLECTION?

Gardner (2014) argues that there are a range of definitions of reflection and recognises that it requires further exploration and research to clearly identify how it can best meet social work practioners' needs. However, she is clear that whichever method of reflection or critical reflection engages you, it is critical for your development to reflect. She argues that critical reflection is the understanding of how external factors influence both your practice and the service user's responses. Similarly, Fook (2014) suggests that critical reflection to develop an understanding of how the social, cultural and economic factors impact upon service provision, service users and our practice is imperative. Whilst reflection on your skill development is beneficial, it is through critical reflection that you will gain the most holistic understanding and therefore development of your social work skills.

Reflective Task 6.2

After your next lecture, as you are commuting home allow yourself the luxury of thinking about the lecture. What is the theme that keeps coming to the forefront of your mind?

What is the interesting issue that makes you smile or consider it further? Why is this engaging you? How could you explore the idea further?

What was the area that you did not quite understand and are having to think harder about? Why did you find it difficult? How could you understand it differently?

This is reflecting. You do it every day without realising it. If you see reflecting as the thinking about the things that are important to you or 'bugging' you, reflecting demystifies it and makes it more achievable. However, it is also significantly more complex and challenging. Your social work reflections (written and oral) should incorporate understanding of your self; understanding of others' behaviours; knowledge of social work theories and models of intervention; knowledge of social work policy and legislation; and consideration of your own values and other's perspectives. Whilst you may not address every one of these areas in every one of your reflections, they need to be evident across your placement reflections as a whole.

POTENTIAL PLACEMENT *PITFALL* Angela wrote excellent reflections each week (as proscribed by her university) on her interventions with others. She was able to reflect on why another professional had been oppressive, the service user's limited capacity to change, and the problem with the social work system. However, despite feedback and advice from her practice educator she failed to look at herself within the reflections, and the practice educator was unable to evaluate Angela's understanding of herself and her development.

POTENTIAL PLACEMENT *OPPORTUNITY* Njeri wrote excellent reflections each week (as proscribed by her university) on her interventions with others. She varied her focus each week, so that her practice educator could see, and Njeri could evidence, a breadth of her development in a wide range of areas.

A reflection asks you to look at yourself and your practice, and that can be hard. You have to be open to give yourself and accept praise to enable you to build on your strengths. By acknowledging what you did well in a difficult circumstance you will build your resilience and confidence to deal with future difficult situations. You also have to be open to your own and others' constructive criticism of your practice and reflecting on its merits. By recognising where you could have *done better*, reflecting on why it happened the way it happened, and considering different ways to approach the situation, you enhance your practice for future interventions. Nevertheless, Sicora (2019) warns against developing only an inward reflective style, arguing that it can become critical rather than developmental, and advocates a more holistic reflective technique for social work students.

Chapter 3 provides a useful discussion on engaging a service user, and asks you to consider how their previous experiences may impact on their responses to you (e.g. empathic reflection), but also how your ability to communicate can influence their reactions to your intervention. In reflections you also need to reflect on other people's behaviours, reactions and perspectives. Mantell (2019) argues that your reflections can be enhanced by incorporating your service users' feelings and views. If you understand their perspective, then you can adjust your intervention and communication to best engage them. For example, if someone is angry and frustrated, an assertive approach may be less effective than a placatory but clear approach.

Reflection also requires you to understand the *why*. Chapter 9 looks at assignment writing and the application of theory to practice, but it is very important that within a reflection you apply your knowledge to your discussion. It is only by understanding why it went well or how it could be enhanced that your practice will develop.

Reflective Task 6.3

Theodore misuses alcohol and had successfully been accessing support from his local substance misuse team. However, he unexpectedly returns to his previous drinking patterns, and attends your placement some weeks later for support.

How will you offer him support?

This reflective task is not to measure your knowledge of substance misuse treatments, but to illustrate that, whatever your placement, you may come across a situation that necessitates some understanding beyond your placement's presenting service provision. Whilst a student in a substance misuse team may be able to reflect on the need for motivational interviewing strategy (Miller and Rollnick, 1991) to engage Theodore effectively, other service users may require a less specialised approach. Certainly, understanding of the transtheoretical model of behaviour change (Prochaska and DiClemente, 1983) will enhance your understanding of the most appropriate response and intervention to support Theodore's recovery, and knowledge of the local services will enable you to signpost the correct services. Furthermore, knowing and understanding your placement team's core model will enable you to practice in that way, so a placement that promotes restorative practice would provide a challenging and supportive response to Theodore.

It is only by developing an understanding of a range of social work theories and models that you will be able to assess *how* to best support him.

Additionally, your knowledge about the relevant procedures, social policy and legislation and how they can be applied to your intervention will be relevant to your reflection. Gardner (2014) argues that as a social worker we may face difficult ethical dilemmas where our social work values contrast with our agency policies and need to examine decisions through a critical lens. The task of researching a procedure for your reflection will enhance your knowledge and understanding of the system, enabling your practice to be of a better standing. Consider how they can be used for positive intervention (e.g. to safeguard a child), but also whether there are ethical dilemmas that arise from rigid boundaries.

Reflective Task 6.4

Reflect on the limitations on service provision for a vulnerable service user imposed by an agency's service provision criteria or on the power that a relevant legislation provides you with.

What are the key factors?

Is there a conflict between your social work values and your need to adhere to your agency criteria?

Can you identify your values?

An important reflection is the understanding of the context of your placement: what oppression may a service user have experienced because of their minority status? If you consider Thompson's (1992) PCS analysis model, whilst a service user may have experienced personal oppression and abuse because of a cultural label that may impact on their confidence and self-esteem, this may have been compounded by structural decisions that denied them access to necessary services or enforced unwanted services on to them. Understanding how service provision across your geographical area interacts will help you to understand different professional perspectives and priorities.

Within reflections, you should also consider your values. Thompson (2016) argues that our values can become stagnant if we do not continue to reflect upon them, putting at yourself risk of becoming discriminatory as you become a qualified social worker. As Chapter 5 discussed, your personal and professional values will have developed as you have progressed through your social work course. You will have been asked to think about why you think that way, or why you hold a value dear. This should continue exponentially in placement, as your expectations and beliefs are challenged against reality. Do not be afraid in a reflection to express or explore your values development, stating that you had an inappropriate initial reactions but that you explored it, will not cause concern but rather demonstrate your growth. It is only by asking yourself why that you are open to exploring alternative values or affirming your existing values. Indeed, Gardner (2014) argues that your self-esteem can be developed through development of integrity and values, a sense of knowing that by debating an ethical dilemma you understand that your decision making was grounded in strong professional values can strengthen your emotional resilience.

▬▬▬ Seven Strategies to Strengthen your Reflective Writing Style ▬▬▬

1   Always write in the first person: own your feelings, values and perspective.
2   Reduce the amount of description you provide: the reader wants to understand how you feel about it, not what happened.
3   Vary the content of your reflections across the placement, so that you demonstrate your skill development, your values, the context in which you practice and an empathic and theoretical understanding of others.
4   Support your reflection with theory where you can, but do not allow it to stop you from reflecting.

5   Be creative if reflective writing is not your strength: use diagrams and charts, or speak into a dictaphone, to express your thoughts then build from there.
6   Use your practice educator to develop how you reflect on ideas, both verbally in supervision and through feedback on written reflections.
7   Use university support and training to enhance your skills: they have lots of practical help to enhance your skills.

A good reflection, be it verbal, written or thought, incorporates consideration of a number of issues, but most importantly focuses on you, on your development and on your understanding of your self. Schon (1983) argues that there are two levels of reflection: the reflection that happens as the event is occurring, *in action*; and the reflection that happens after the event, *on action*. In no way does this chapter seek to minimise the importance of reflection in action, which Ferguson (2018) argues is essential for critically analysing and assessing a situation to ensure optimum outcomes by altering your intervention. Nevertheless, the focus is most definitely on how to reflect on action. I would argue that by enhancing your ability to reflect on action that your ability to reflect in action will consequently be improved.

HOW TO REFLECT?

Collecting all of those ideas and putting them onto paper can be difficult, so using a reflective model can be a helpful way to organise your thinking. This section of the chapter will reflect on different models of reflection. An important point to remember throughout is that a reflection is not about illustrating to your practice educator only your successes, but that the greatest learning can be found from those experiences that were challenging for you, and explored reflectively can enhance your understanding and skills as you move forward in placement. Your practice educator will be enabled to identify your areas for development and aid you in that development if you are open and honest in your reflections.

As you read through this section, consider each reflective model in turn and reflect upon an intervention using its principles. Please feel free to use your own example, or use one of the following ideas:

- At the end of the first day of placement reflect on how you felt about the learning opportunities that will be available to you.
- After attending an inter-professional meeting, compare and contrast how you engaged the service user and professionals.
- After a straightforward home visit, how could you have enhanced your practice?
- After a difficult home visit, what issues contributed to it being difficult?

By using the same example with each model of reflection, you will be able to develop an understanding of which one suits your learning style the best.

Many universities provide a range of reflective proformas, and they can be exceptionally helpful as you start to reflect, but do have the confidence to recognise their limitations. As you develop your reflective writing skills you may grow beyond the formulaic proformas and be able to write freely, yet within the confines of a relatively small word limit. Irrespective of the model chosen, remember that you need to provide a brief description of the event to allow word allocation to the critical analysis of the event, covering the areas discussed above. Your practice educator wants to see a depth of discussion to illustrate your understanding of events and your development. It will often be the starting point of a collaborative discussion that enables both yourself and your practice educator to explore it further.

Arguably the simplest model is Driscoll's (2007) 'What?' model, where the student is asked:

What? A concise description of the event: what happened?

So what? An exploration of why something happened, using the ideas above to reflect on why your intervention went well or needed to be enhanced. So what impacted on you and others?

Now what? Your learning from the event and any tasks that arise from it. Now what will you do with your new understanding?

Using the intervention identified above, consider:

What?

So what?

Now what?

Similarly straightforward are the '4 F's', which ask the student to consider the *facts*, their *feelings* and *findings* to develop a *future* (Greenaway, 2014, cited in Maclean et al., 2018), and Jasper's (2003, cited in Bassot, 2016) ERA model, which recommends *experience*, *reflection* and *action*. Finally, Fook and Gardner (2007) provide a two-stage model for critical reflection. Stage one is analysis/exploration/deconstruction, and stage two is change/reconstruction, to enable you to consider your intervention and plan for enhanced future interventions.

Alternatively, a much-used reflective model is that of Gibbs' (1988) reflective cycle. It sets out a more detailed but similar model to the 'What?' model (Driscoll, 2007). It asks the reflector to briefly *describe* the intervention, then focus on their *feelings* about it. They are asked to *evaluate* what went wrong and what went well, and *analyse* why that might have been. Finally, the reflector is asked to *conclude* their reflection by considering how they could have undertaken it differently, and create an *action plan* to help them to do so next time. The cycle then begins again as the reflector tries a similar intervention and applies the learning from the first incident. Beesley et al. (2018) provide a demonstration of this reflective model in practice.

Reflective Task 6.6

Reflect on your previous intervention using the following headings:

Description

Feelings

Evaluation

Analysis

Conclusion

Action plan

SHARE is a new perspective proposed by Maclean et al. (2018), which can be applied to a reflective model. The reflector is required to consider what did they *see* and what did they *hear* that influenced how they *act*ed, to *read* to understand the service user's needs and the theoretical perspective that underpinned the work, to ensure an evidence-based *evaluation*. Maclean et al. (2018) argue that this approach places the service user at the centre of all your practice, and that your evaluation should take account of professional and structural power dynamics.

Consider your intervention using the following parameters. What did you:

See

Hear

Act

Read

Evaluate

Before placement your tutor, either individual or within a module, will have given you support and direction about reflective writing, and your university is likely to have additional support in the form of e-tutorials to access. Develop your reflective skills whilst you have a little more space to develop a reflective routine, so that when your placement begins you have an established routine to support you.

REFLECTIVE SUPERVISION

Whilst a written reflection often focuses on your perspective, oral reflection in formal or informal supervision can incorporate both your own perspective and those of your practice educator. A common feature of supervision is feedback on your practice, which can lead to productive reflective discussions that enable you to consider your practice and learning needs. The Johari Window (Luft and Ingham, 1955) reminds you that you cannot always see the skills that you have yet to develop, and that feedback facilitates that process of identification, which then enables action. Chapter 7 will support your processing of constructive feedback, but remember the power of positive feedback to enhance your confidence and self-esteem for future interventions. Kuusisaari (2014) argues that collaborative work enables the student to hear and reflect upon the practice educator's perspectives and ideas, and question and clarify their meaning without fear of repercussion, resulting in an ability to work together to problem solve.

Green and Crisp (2007) reflect on the positive use of a critical incident analysis in social work student supervision to aid learning from reflection. They argue that although initially created to reflect on major incidents such as aviation disasters, Tripp (1993) developed the reflection on learning from daily incidents, both productive and those with less favourable outcomes, to consider how the student's existing values and knowledge can be applied to the incident to develop greater understanding. Within supervision the practice educator would work collaboratively to make suggestions and explore different perspectives. Their research concluded that a structure for reflection and critical analysis greatly aided the students' development.

Reflective Task 6.7 (continued)

Consider the values and knowledge that you used within the reflective incident:

Account of the incident

Initial responses to the incident

Issues and dilemmas highlighted from the incident

Learning

Outcomes

(Green and Crisp, 2007)

Papouli (2016) concurred that the use of a critical incident analysis tool aided a social work student's development of their understanding of their professional values.

Creative approaches to reflection that link to your learning style will enhance your learning. Techniques to consider include, as discussed in Chapter 5, Collingwood (2005) who provides a framework for enhancing your application of theory to reflecting on your practice in supervision, or a spider diagram to plot out your areas for discussion and adding further bubbles to highlight subsections. Furthermore, Collen (2019) argues that workshops that involve service users to explore ethical dilemmas enhance empathic and reflective thinking. Whilst you may not have access to formal workshops, as discussed in Chapter 4, undertaking meaningful and interactive discussion to gain service user feedback to understand their perspective can only enhance your reflective skills, understanding and development.

As with service user interventions, reflective approaches are not 'one size fits all', and you should spend time exploring the reflective style that benefits you. Time spent reflecting in a style that suits you, both individually and in supervision, can only benefit your practice and enhance your social work skills and knowledge. What may start as a 'means to an end' task for university should become an entrenched skill that supports your practice and development throughout your career.

■■■■ **PLACEMENT PERSPECTIVE 6.2** ■■■■

Student's perspective on reflections

Developing critical reflections was a real struggle for me. Whilst on placement I found it hard to establish a balance between home life, academic work and placement tasks. I would always prioritise my responsibilities on placement as I did not want

to do the service users an injustice, therefore writing reflections were always placed at the bottom of my list of priorities. I didn't do a reflection every two weeks as I should have done, therefore towards the end of placement I felt overwhelmed with worry, which negatively impacted upon my grades. In retrospect, I realised that not keeping up to date with my reflections meant that service users were not receiving best practice from me anyway as I was not reflecting on my practice to better it. My advice would be to reflect regularly as it really does maximise your learning; you could do this by simply keeping a diary and writing in it at break times, even if it is something small as a reminder for you to reflect on.

Hannah Cunningham, BA Social Work Student

CHAPTER SUMMARY

Reflection is a critical part of your social work student placement development. Whilst your university may proscribe a set amount of written reflections per placement, you should see it as an important daily exercise that enables you to understand your role and enhance your practice. Whilst it will, at first, be a task that necessitates following a structured format, with practice it will become a natural task that you undertake after every intervention or incident, as you drive back to the office or write up case notes.

Reflection should use a strengths perspective: build on your strengths to give you confidence to address your areas for development. It should reflect on what happened, based on your skills, knowledge and values, and why it happened, to enable you to develop a plan for future interventions.

CHAPTER CHECKLIST

In order to develop your reflective skills, it is helpful to:

✔ try different reflective techniques and identify one that best suits your learning style
✔ ensure that you reflect on your own development
✔ reflect on a service user's perspective to enhance your empathy
✔ understand the 'why' of how things work by applying theory to your reflection
✔ consider your professional value base and how that influences your practice.

Further reading

Chapter 1 'Reflection and emotional intelligence', in Beesley, P., Watts, M. and Harrison, M. (2018) *Developing Your Communication Skills in Social Work*. London: SAGE.

Collingwood, P (2005) 'Integrating theory and practice: the three-stage theory framework', *Journal of Practice Teaching*, 6 (1): 6–23.

Fook, J. (2014) *Social Work: A Critical Approach to Practice*. London: SAGE.

Gardner, F. (2014) *Being Critically Reflective*. London: Palgrave.

Mantell, A. and Scragg, T (2019) *Reflective Practice in Social Work*. London: SAGE

7

RESPONDING POSITIVELY TO CONSTRUCTIVE FEEDBACK

This chapter will reflect on how to respond positively when your practice educator provides you with constructive feedback. This may be that you need to address developmental areas to consolidate and enhance your practice, or it may be that the progress on placement is not going as planned. It will consider the expectations on a social work student, and what good enough practice is. It will offer advice throughout to the student, with a clear focus on the need to reflect on their own practice to enhance their holistic skills and capability, whilst utilising collaborative learning with the practice educator. The philosophy is to aid the reader to identify ways to avoid the placement situation deteriorating further, but will also consider the ultimate outcome of a failed placement.

◼◼◼◼ PLACEMENT PERSPECTIVE 7.1 ◼◼◼◼

Practice educator's perspective on the importance of social work students engaging when concerns are raised

Part of our continuing learning is to be able take on board constructive feedback. This is not always easy but is a key part of promoting good practice. I would want the student to be the best they can be, both in the placement and beyond. Concerns may arise in placement for a number of reasons, including around student progress or performance. As part of supporting a student in passing their placement, it is important that any concerns are raised as they become apparent.

My experience as a practice educator reinforces to me the importance of open and honest dialogue from the start from all parties.

My initial approach to working to address issues would be to undertake a direct discussion with the student. We talk a lot in social work about maintaining good communication with our service users but this is equally important within the supervisory working relationship. I would

(Continued)

hope that if I was to note concerns regarding student progress or performance that the student themselves would also have identified such issues. This highlights the importance of reflective practice and using tools such as supervision and reflective writing to support this process. Upon hearing the concerns, I would expect a student to reflect upon the issues and use the information as a springboard upon which to base their continued learning.

Collaborative learning is one of the reasons I enjoy the practice educator role as I appreciate the focus of learning together. However, this can only occur if both the practice educator and the student are committed to the relationship and to the process. This means that I would look for the student to be motivated to learn and be proactive in their learning. I would want to work with the student so that together we could identify the practical steps that could be undertaken in order to work toward the presenting concerns. This would include the actions the student would need to undertake, but also identify the support to be provided by the practice educator and placement agency.

I feel it is critical to maintain open and regular dialogue and I would expect the student to take a joint lead in this with myself. It is in the student's interest to identify and discuss issues as soon as possible in the placement journey in order to give themselves the greatest time and opportunity to address the issues. I appreciate that there is a power imbalance in the practice educator/ student working relationship, but in assessing a student I am focused not just on the presenting issue but, and perhaps more importantly, also upon how the student reflects and responds to the issue.

Discussion is only one step in addressing the concerns. Discussion should lead to active steps being undertaken. My expectation would be for the student to proactively action the identified change. As a practice educator I would willingly support a student through this process, but it is the student who will would need to evidence the change that means they are able to move forward.

Nicky Linacre, Off-site Practice Educator

As discussed in Chapter 3, your relationship with your practice educator is key to a successful social work student placement. You will require an open dialogue to successfully navigate the pitfalls, problems, joys, conundrums and successes that you encounter on placement. A good practice educator will walk with you through your social work journey, model good practice for you and offer you support and advice on your practice to enable collaborative learning. It is a normal practice educator task to give constructive feedback to a student throughout placement to enable them to identify and address areas for development. Finch (2017: 71) advocates the necessity of 'courageous conversations' whereby practice educators provide open and honest feedback to support students' development. You will need to be open to seeking and receiving support and constructive feedback from your practice educator to enhance your practice and to taking steps to address the issues raised.

WHAT IS GOOD ENOUGH PRACTICE?

Every social work body has an expected level of practice that a social work student is expected to demonstrate. In the UK, BASW (2018) provide different levels of capability within the PCF for different levels of social work student study, and these have been used throughout this book as the standards upon which you will work towards. Your practice educator will assess your practice against these standards and offer you positive and constructive feedback to enable you to understand how you are progressing on placement. By understanding the expectations upon you, you are making a proactive approach towards avoiding the F-word (fail).

However, standards provide guidelines only. They are not basic skills and requirements that once achieved can allow you to relax, but instead should be seen as *minimums* that you need to undertake to pass your placement. You need to demonstrate progress as a social work student on placement, irrespective of your starting point. If you have engaged with the philosophy of this book, just good enough is not enough for you. I advocate that you need to work hard to be the *best* social work student that you can be, whatever level that may be. As with the rest of the book, this chapter will help you to develop your social work practice effectively and maximise your potential.

So, what is *good enough* practice? As a social worker you need to demonstrate good professionalism and intervention skills, but also the knowledge to support why you undertake your intervention and the ability to critically reflect on your skills, supported throughout by strong social work values. As a social work student, you will need to demonstrate a holistic approach to your placement that demonstrates a developing ability within *all* of these areas. Chapters 5 and 6 have discussed how to ensure that you engage with each of these abilities, and I will refer you back to those as you read through this chapter.

POTENTIAL PLACEMENT *PITFALL* Scarlett was a strong academic student. She was able to discuss with her practice educator the theories that she used when she started to undertake interventions with service users. However, she did not complete any reflections, and in supervision could not identify how she was feeling or why service users might react as they did.

Her practice educator raised concerns in supervision that Scarlett was not able to critically reflect. This began to impact on her ability to complete assessments and for Scarlett to develop her skills, which resulted in an action plan meeting being called to support her thinking. The tutor organised for Scarlett to attend mindfulness classes at university, but Scarlett did not engage with it. The practice educator did reflection development exercises in supervision, but Scarlett did not complete her reflections as she found them difficult. Eventually Scarlett failed her placement as she could not demonstrate capability in critical analysis and reflection.

POTENTIAL PLACEMENT *OPPORTUNITY* Lily was a strong academic student. She was able to discuss with her practice educator the theories that she used when she started to undertake interventions with service users. However, she did not complete any reflections, and in supervision could not identify how she was feeling or why service users might react as they did.

Her practice educator raised concerns in supervision that Lily was not able to critically reflect, and together they engaged in tasks to develop the skill. Lily found this very hard but was committed to developing her skills and made progress. As a qualified social worker, Lily finds that reflection has become more natural, and benefits her understanding of a service user's motivations and behaviours.

If you are open to reflecting on your practice, you will have won half the battle. Every social work student will have areas for development raised with them and need to respond positively to further their learning. Lomax and Jones (2014) recognise that positive feedback feeds our confidence and enthusiasm, but that constructive feedback may not be as agreeable. It is inevitable that you will be given constructive feedback as part of your placement. This is not because your practice educator likes to spread misery, but because one of their roles is to educate: and it is only by giving you constructive feedback to help you to recognise the areas that you need to develop that they can support you to develop your skills.

CONCERNS PROCESSES

If a practice educator has concerns about your practice, there are a series of processes that they need to follow, which should be seen as opportunities for you to engage with the placement, reflect on concerns and enhance your skills in order to be successful. It should be noted that not all of these will necessarily be followed, as if concerns are immediate and serious, it may be that the placement is suspended pending investigation, or that having raised informal concerns, the issues are addressed and there is no further need for this process.

SHARE INFORMAL CONCERNS IN SUPERVISION IN A TIMELY AND EVIDENCE-BASED MANNER

Supervision should be a forum for your practice educator and yourself to discuss all positives and areas for development, as discussed in Chapter 3. This means that it is the correct time and place for your practice educator to first raise concerns about your practice or progress. Feedback should be given to you as quickly as possible (Race, 2007), using clear examples of your practice and the areas to be developed. In my experience, many students who go on social work placement will experience some level of constructive feedback on placement about areas that need to be enhanced, so this should be seen as productive to your development. At this point you need to be *open* to hearing the concerns.

------| **Reflective Task 7.1** |--

How do you respond to feedback?

Do you have a fight or flight response? Do you listen passively and agree, then disregard it, demonstrating disguised compliance? Are you initially closed, but go away and think about things away from the situation?

....

It is important to recognise that we will all have coping strategies that defend us from criticism or feedback. However, time reflecting on areas that you need to address now will prevent you continuing down this process and so avoids stress and enhances your practice, making you a better social worker in the long run.

An important element of being a social worker is the ability to take constructive feedback, reflect on issues raised, and make changes to enhance your practice. If you find this difficult now, the skill you need to develop is both the skill on which you have received feedback and the skill of accepting and reflecting on feedback. It is not the mistake that fails you but your response to it that determines the practice educator's response. If you can hear the area for development and demonstrate progress, you will be praised, whilst if you become defensive and refuse to acknowledge any need to develop, then inevitably your practice educator will have more concerns about you. Doel (2010) discusses the importance of *mindset*, arguing that when things are difficult a student can choose to embrace the concerns as a learning opportunity or can choose to be defensive and blame others for their failure. A positive mindset will enable you to move forward positively by being open to support and your own development.

Most of the time, this constructive feedback will be an area of development that the practice educator has identified that you need extra support and education to develop. You may be aware of it as an area to develop, and be both happy and relieved to accept the support as it will enhance your performance and success of the placement. Indeed, Davys and Beddoe (2010, cited in Fenge et al., 2014) say that if feedback is requested it is received well. Sadler (2010) argues that feedback is often seen as the mentor *telling* the student their strengths and areas for development, and argues that without depth of understanding the student will not engage in a change of behaviour, which is why self-evaluation, as discussed in the direct observation stage, is critical. By working collaboratively with you, your practice educator can support you to understand yourself and identify the need for, and therefore action, change.

Fenge et al. (2014) reflect that you may have to work with your practice educator on understanding the difference between how you see your practice and how the practice educator sees it. In my experience, a student who works through differences with their practice educator often learns most about themselves in the process of enhancing their practice, whilst those who are closed to learning are likely to be unsuccessful in placement.

> Difficult experiences can enhance … problem-solving skills, assist … to identify and understand … strengths and areas for development, and enable … [you]… to act in ways which can contribute to successful outcomes. (Tedam, 2015: 140)

Reflective Task 7.2

Think back to a time when you were struggling to learn a new skill – learning to drive or a new language, for instance.

What motivated you to keep trying? What techniques helped you to 'get it'?

You are the expert in yourself. I can tell you a thousand times that 'you write with your right and the one that is left is left', but until you find a way that is meaningful for you, it will not help you to remember your left from your right. Discuss with your practice educator the best way to maximise your learning. They will be impressed with both your self-awareness and your motivation to work through the concern. An impressed practice educator will always be an invested practice educator, and together you are more likely to pass placement.

SHARE FORMAL CONCERN IN SUPERVISION IN A TIMELY AND EVIDENCE-BASED MANNER

Whilst all the issues above remain valid at this point, the practice educator will make these more formal by discussion of concerns and required actions in supervision. You should ensure that you understand the concerns, the areas for development and the expectations upon you to demonstrate progress. A practice educator will never criticise you for asking for clarity as it shows engagement and commitment to the change process.

Sennett (2008) argues that challenging incidents can be used by the mentor as stimulating learning opportunities. He promotes the use of reframing a problem to find a solution. He argues that the mentor's role is to support the student to consider the obstacle from a variety of perspectives to help them to identify the best way for them to approach the problem and resolve it effectively. If your practice educator empowers you to reach a solution, you will be equipped with the knowledge, understanding and skills to transfer this to another future situation.

I would reiterate that you can stop the concerns process at this point by engaging with the practice educator and demonstrating change, as that is all they are looking for.

ACTION PLAN MEETING

If there are immediate concerns from a significant example of poor practice, or if the practice educator has raised concerns through supervision but not evidenced any development, an action plan meeting (sometimes called a 'concerns meeting') will be called. This can be called by yourself as the student, or the practice educator or the tutor. Whilst clearly this will not fill you with delight, try to see it as an opportunity to get the help *you* need to pass *your* placement. An action plan meeting should discuss the concerns, again citing evidence-based examples of your practice, highlight what you need to demonstrate for you to be on track to pass your placement, and will provide clear criteria on the help that you will receive from practice educator, placement and university to help you achieve this. It is up to you how you engage with this meeting, but a collaborative approach to addressing concerns is always more effective.

Reflective Task 7.3

You have undertaken a home visit to a service user who is either uncommunicative or angry. How do you feel about the service user? Do you feel that they are committed to working with you? Do you feel that they are likely to change?

What about a service user who is open with you and trying to make changes in their life?

Now think about how you present in your action plan meeting. How do you want your practice educator to see you? Do you need to reflect upon your attitude to best engage the practice educator to support you?

Sadly, it is human nature to work harder to support someone who is trying to help themselves. Your goal here is to invest in yourself so that your practice educator is also invested in you. You want to work with them to get the best possible support so that you can make the most of your placement learning opportunities and turn the concerns into capabilities. To do this, you need to attend this meeting open to the concerns that will be reviewed, having prepared by reflecting on the concerns and identified ways in which you can seek support and develop your skills, and both listen and express your thoughts so that you are actively participant in the meeting.

Boddy et al. (2018) discuss the importance of hope in social work relationships. They propose that a social worker's hope facilitates the ability to support and motivate change in others. If this is related to the practice educator/social work student relationship, it can be seen that if the practice educator hopes you can do it, motivated by your commitment to change, that you will begin to believe in yourself and be more likely to achieve. This relationship will be crucial if you are facing concerns on placement, the ability to work collaboratively to resolve the concerns with hope, motivation and commitment together.

REVIEW ACTION PLAN MEETING

At the action plan meeting your tutor should agree a date to review the action, usually four to six weeks later. This review meeting will consider your commitment and your progress to addressing the concerns, which means that you need to have shown immediate and consistent addressing of the concerns. If you have done this, then your practice educator will recognise the development, and assess your progress. Beckett (1983: 1) reminds us that we can only do our best: 'Ever tried? Ever failed? No matter. Try again. Fail again. Fail better.'

Your practice educator wants to see that you are learning from the feedback and making progress. It may be that there is need for a further review meeting, or that this ends the concerns. Of course, if you have not shown any commitment or skill development, then the tutor and practice educator will need to discuss whether your placement remains viable.

TERMINATE PLACEMENT

You can work hard to prevent yourself from failing by engaging in the processes above. However, if a student does not demonstrate progress in the skills identified despite support offered, or shows no commitment to placement learning, then the practice educator can decide that the student has not shown capability on placement, which is deemed a failed placement. Similarly, if a student demonstrates poor practice that puts themselves, colleagues or service users at risk, the placement can be suspended immediately, pending reflection on terminating the placement.

It is a practice educator's duty to fail students who are not able to demonstrate capability in all the areas of social work, including intervention skills, values, reflection and ability to put theory into practice. Social work is a professional body that must ensure that its workforce practices are to a good enough standard to meet the needs of vulnerable service users.

However, it is incredibly hard on all involved when a student fails placement. The practice educator may perceive that they have let you down and feel guilty (Finch and Taylor 2013). It is likely that you will feel a range of emotions, from anger to grief, from rejection to failure. It is important that you allow yourself to explore these emotions and give yourself time to reflect on the placement experience. Arrange to meet with your tutor and explore the consequences of the placement decision, as each university has a different perspective from here. Lomax and Jones (2014) advise you to refer you to your module, course and university procedures to determine your future options and make an informed decision, and Edmondson (2014) reminds us that your students union will offer support and advice if you feel that you need to contest a negative placement outcome.

However, irrespective of the different procedural response, take time to reflect on maintaining sight of your strengths and skills that you developed on placement, whilst also recognising and accepting the areas for development that you still have. A placement termination should be seen as not yet good enough. With time, and university support, to develop your identified learning needs and skills, you may be assessed as ready to undertake another placement, which you can consider the second half of the same placement, an opportunity to further develop the skills you began to develop in the first placement. Tedam (2015) argues that a social work student can have a positive experience yet fail their placement if the learning journey has been facilitated by working towards building confidence and competence collaboratively with your practice educator to meet your individualised needs.

WRONG TIME, WRONG PLACE, WRONG CAREER

Nicholas and Kerr (2015) recognise that factors which impact on a student's ability can be personal factors, skill set and academic issues, whilst they may also be influenced by the practice educator's skill set, oppressive practice (by practice educator or team), wider agency problems, or inadequate academic support. In my experience as a tutor and previously a practice educator of many social work students on placement, I have found that there are three main areas why a social work student has significant concerns raised about them and is unable to address them to avoid their placement being terminated. Most fails can be avoided by the student if they are able to reflect on their input into the process. But, as we will discuss, that is easier said than done. Most often these reasons are wrong time, wrong place, or wrong career choice.

....: **Reflective Task 7.4** :......

As you read through this section, spend some time and reflect upon whether you can identify if you have any blocks to your learning. Consider if you need to discuss them with your practice educator or tutor to identify ways to address them.

The first reason that social work students' practice is not good enough is that the student has a level of personal issues that are impacting on their practice and emotional wellbeing. As we discussed in Chapter 3, if you have personal issues such as health, caring responsibilities or having suffered a bereavement or relationship breakdown, it is critical that you alert both your tutor and your practice educator so that they can offer you advice and support. However, it is your choice to continue on placement, and a significant number of students who have concerns raised about them on placement have either undisclosed or ignored personal issues, which are impacting on their practice. If you recognise that this might be you, stop and think on a little harder. Greer (2016: 35) reflects that resilient social workers need to have self-confidence and self-esteem, but also that:

> an important aspect of resilience ... is being able to admit that we are feeling
> overwhelmed and need help.

There is nothing wrong with admitting it is not working for you today, and asking for help, a break in placement, or even stopping the placement until the following year. I would call this an emotionally intelligent decision. In social work we have to make complex decisions about service users lives and therefore we have to be *fit to practice* (HCPC, 2016).

The second reason that a social work student may experience difficulties on placement is that the placement *fit* does not quite work. This may be that the placement was not what you expected, though this is not an acceptable reason to go on to fail placement. If you are not allocated your dream placement and feel angry that your friend was, you will need to resolve this immediately as you are the block to learning here. Knowles (1973) discusses the criteria for successful adult learning, and one of the key principles is that the learner must be open to learning.

This is not to say that everything is your fault, but the first step to change is to identify and accept that you need to change. Prochaska and DiClemente (1983) identify that in order to make changes in your behaviour, you need to *contemplate* them before you can take *action*. Whilst writing initially about how service users addressed substance misuse, their findings are applicable to any change one makes and are invaluable here for you to start to recognise that it is your placement and that *you* need to make changes to fulfil an assessed criterion. If you want to make your learning more effective, by identifying an area that is blocking your learning and making adaptations to enhance your approach to learning, you will only benefit from the reflection.

However, there are also occasions when wrong place is because the *fit* between social work student and practice educator is not working as well as it should. Doel (2010) recognises that this can be because of different cultural backgrounds, be that ethnicity, age, gender and so on, or different learning styles, and recommends talking to each other as a solution. Obviously, the practice educator needs to reflect and develop different techniques to engage you in the learning process, but equally you have to work to address this incongruent relationship. It is recognised that there are issues of power that the social work student faces within this that complicate the situation and make it more difficult. However, you do need to self-advocate that it is not working for you, and to work through the problem with your practice educator. Conflict resolution is a key component of being a social worker.

Reflective Task 7.5

If you recognise that your relationship with your practice educator is not supporting your development, how will you raise this with them? What strategies can you employ to engage your practice educator? How can you be different to change this relationship?

The dual concern model (developed from work by Blake and Mouton, 1964) acknowledges that each person's style of conflict resolution is based on their own understanding of, and ability to assert, their own needs balanced against their empathy for the other person's needs. This argues that dependent on whose needs you see as more important will determine your approach to conflict resolution, including avoidance, accommodating, competitive, conciliation or co-operation styles, and will vary dependent on the situation. The best approach, then, is to balance and prioritise, ensuring that your needs are heard and valued with an understanding of the other person's perspective in a co-operative style. The key element for me here is communication, communication, communication, to paraphrase a popular television show.

Reflective Task 7.5 (continued)

How do you consider that the practice educator might be feeling if the placement is not going well? Practice your empathy skills here and reflect upon their disappointment and feelings of failure. Can you use this to engage them and work together to address this?

As a student you may be feeling powerless to challenge your practice educator. Criticism may lower your self-esteem and self-confidence, or make you feel angry at the unfairness, and confused as to what you need to do to demonstrate your ability. If you can negotiate an outcome using the styles suggested, you will be demonstrating both your emotional resilience to resolve conflict and your professionalism, but more importantly will have enhanced your placement, learning and outcomes as a result.

If you have tried to address the problems with your practice educator but feel that you are making no progress, then you should talk to your tutor and ask for advice and support.

The final area where a social work student may struggle is when they are not suitable to become a social worker. This is incredibly rare. However, despite stringent admissions processes, tutor input and assessments, sometimes a social work student can experience their placement as a time to explore what social work actually is. If you recognise that social work is not as you thought, I would recommend discussions with your practice educator and tutor to identify if the time has come to consider alternative career options. Lomax and Jones (2014) advise that you discuss academic credits and alternative academic qualifications to ensure that you gain recognition from the work undertaken. The option of a change in career is not about failure; instead it is about recognising who you are and making an emotionally intelligent decision to use your strengths in a different area. Unfortunately, sometimes the practice educator recognises this before you do, and may undertake work to help you identify this.

Alternatively, it can be that the student does not possess the right attributes required to be a proficient social worker. Social workers are required to be empathic, assertive, proactive, authoritative, organised, to name but a few essential skills. Not all of these skills come naturally to everyone who applies to become a social work student, and Finch (2017: 32) reminds us that sometimes social work students have to 'unlearn' habits and values. Whilst that collaborative learning between practice educator and student can support the student to explore their anxiety about letting go of old strategies in favour of new, more productive ones, there are a few people for whom their skills, attributes or values do not align with social work practice. You will need to reflect on your suitability, which can be a difficult process as it will require an open and honest introspection. Of course, if you do not realise this, and continue to demonstrate insufficient capacity in some or all areas, your practice educator has a duty to fail your placement, sometimes before the end of your placement if you are placing service users at risk. That is not to say withdraw to avoid failure, but instead to ask you to reflect upon if social work is right for you.

━━━━━━━━━━ PLACEMENT PERSPECTIVE 7.2 ━━━━━━━━━━

Student's perspective on turning a failing placement around

Whilst on my final placement my practice educator raised some concerns about my practice as a student social worker, which made me feel anxious. I felt overwhelmed because there were so many concerns raised at the time about my practice, which meant that I had lots of tasks to

(Continued)

complete within a short space of time. I initially started doubting my abilities to accomplish this. I often went into panic mode as I felt I would be unable to meet these deadlines to be able to pass my course and placement. In the past, I often dealt with such situations by withdrawing or by being defensive, but by reflecting on these experiences I had developed my emotional resilience. I was able to use positive thinking and an optimistic attitude to accept these constructive criticisms. I was able to manage the concerns by maintaining an open mind.

Myself, the practice educator and my tutor drew up an action plan, which I used as a guide to work on the areas of concern. I started by prioritising my work. I used a diary and a to-do list which helped me to record my progress. I made sure that I read broadly and I applied the knowledge in practice and started noticing that my skills improved. With this progress, I felt more confident and motivated to continue to work hard. I used the support from the university. My tutor was very supportive and I found my lecture notes very useful as they helped me to focus my reading to the main areas needed for my placement. My practice educator's support was crucial. He helped me to identify my areas of improvement, and supported me to frequently discuss my cases in supervision. This further motivated me on placement.

I was able to persist and pass by challenging myself beyond my comfort zone and making good use of the learning opportunities available on placement.

Maryann Saviour, ASYE

CHAPTER SUMMARY

In conclusion, the need to reflect upon your practice, your skills and your areas to develop underpins the potential success of your social work placement. Social work students do fail on placement, but you can reduce the odds of this happening significantly by engaging with your practice educator and reflecting on your skills. Failure is not inevitable just because your practice educator raises a concern. Take control and face it head-on in a positive way, and you will benefit by developing the skills that you need to be a successful qualified social worker, as well as developing your resilience to survive in a complex and often critical profession.

CHAPTER CHECKLIST

In order to reduce the chances of failing your placement:

✔   listen to any concerns that your practice educator raises and reflect upon them
✔   discuss concerns with your practice educator so that you understand the concerns and what you need to do to address them
✔   ask your practice educator and tutor for support, advice and help, their role is to support you to enhance your skills
✔   reflect if you have any blocks to your learning that could be addressed.

Further reading

Chapter 2 'The psychology of resilience', in Greer, J. (2016) *Resilience and Personal Effectiveness for Social Workers*. London: SAGE.

Chapter 7 'The going gets tough', in Doel, M. (2010) *Social Work Placements: A Traveller's Guide*. Oxford: Routledge.

8

EVIDENCING YOUR CAPABILITY ON PLACEMENT

This chapter will explore the expectations of compiling an evidence portfolio. It will offer advice on how to do this, including tips, strategies and advice. The chapter will provide examples of how to maximise evidence matching so that your evidence folder represents the breadth of work you have undertaken on placement and represents you well. By examining your learning from work undertaken, you are likely to enhance your development as you connect individual activity into holistic learning and are afforded the opportunity to reflect on your development from it.

■ PLACEMENT PERSPECTIVE 8.1 ■

Practice educator's expectations of a student's evidence

As a rule of the thumb, I expect social work students to provide evidence of the work that they have undertaken themselves or even co-worked, but not the work that they have shadowed. However, it is perfectly fine for a student to reflect on their shadowing experience and use the reflective work to evidence development.

I would like to see a variety of evidence in their portfolio; in this way they will also demonstrate a variety in their learning and the range of work that they have done on placement. I would expect a student to include some of the different assessment or reports they have completed during their course of placement. I do try not to be too rigid, and it is alright for a good piece of

evidence to be used as evidence on more than one domain. This is mainly because the evidence is so good, thoroughly done/researched and it 'hits' more than one domain and therefore should not be 'wasted' by just citing it once. I feel that reflections make good evidence as they show the student's learning.

I am always happy to offer advice to students about what to use, as exampled below, but they do need to do it themselves. Suggestions on how to meet the domains are:

Professionalism: evidence of arranging a meeting, chairing a meeting, confidentiality statement, feedback from service users

(Continued)

and professionals, direct observation where the student has conveyed information in a professional manner.

Values and ethics: reflection that evidences their values such as non-judgmental, upholding someone's dignity, rights or advocating for someone.

Diversity: evidence of a student working hard to overcome or challenge discrimination; for example, a referral form to request for an advocate or interpreter to be involved, referral to a culturally appropriate community group, welfare right referrals and application and so on.

Rights, justice and economic wellbeing: a reflection or assessment extract that evidences their understanding of the effects of oppression, discrimination and poverty through reflections, an advocating letter, or a PIP or ESA application.

Knowledge: completed assessments that cite the legal framework or research on which the decision was based, supervision minutes where social work theories were discussed, reflections that cite theory, and training certificates.

Critical reflection and analysis: supervision notes when they were reflecting on a piece

of work and any of their reflections, or an assessment that have required critical analysis to produce a recommendation of service provision.

Intervention and skills: all quality paperwork produced by the student including assessments, support plans, letters, referrals, meeting minutes, as well as the student's direct observations.

Contexts and organisations: understanding structure of service through induction visits, evidence of multi-agency working, referral forms, reflection on different professions' approaches.

Professional leadership: document prepared to present research/feedback on training to team meetings, minutes of meetings chaired by the student social worker, peer support on a piece of work completed, and evidence that they have taken responsibility for their own professional learning and development; for example, certificates of relevant trainings attended with a reflection that shows their learning from it.

Loveworthy Chiguvo, Practice Educator

WHAT IS AN EVIDENCE PORTFOLIO?

Evidence portfolios are used widely across many practical professions as a way for candidates to demonstrate how they have met a set of criteria. It will be important for you to familiarise yourself with your own institution's criteria. Within English social work, evidence is required from each of the PCF domains (BASW, 2018). The PCF is subdivided into career progression levels, the relevant levels for social work students on placement being end of first placement and end of final placement. Within the domains for each level, BASW (2016) provide indicators of how the domain can be evidenced. Some universities ask that you meet each indicator, other universities recommend their use as a guide only. Nevertheless, time spent time familiarising yourself with the domains before and during placement is time well spent (Doel, 2010; Edmondson, 2014; Jones, 2015). Some universities also ask you to match your learning to the *Guidance on Conduct and Ethics for Students* (HCPC, 2017a), *Standards on Proficiency: Social Workers in England*

(HCPC, 2017b) or *Knowledge and Skills Statement for Social Workers in Adult Services* (DoH, 2015) and *Post-qualifying Standard: Knowledge and Skills Statement for Child and Family Practitioners* (DfE, 2018). Each of these are useful documents to familiarise yourself with, whether you are required to match evidence to it or not. Whilst this chapter will use the PCF to demonstrate strategies match evidence, the principles and recommended techniques can be applied to any criteria.

Evidence portfolios may be requested by your university to be handed-in in a physical folder style or within an electronic system. It will be important that you know from the start of placement how your evidence portfolio should be compiled and handed in. A paper folder will require the anonymising and printing of the evidence either for each domain that you intend to use it for, or printing once and providing a numbered portfolio with an evidence grid that directs the reader to the evidence. Mathews et al. (2014) remind us that paper portfolios can become overwhelmingly large, and that good structure is essential for it to be user friendly (practice educator and tutor). An electronic evidence portfolio will require you to know and understand the relevant technology that your university dictates use of. You will be required to save anonymised documents electronically and attach them to specified points. A number of universities use a system called PebblePad, others ask for it in a Word document. However, they will provide support and advice, and all universities have IT support systems for you to access.

Once complete, the evidence portfolio will be given initially to your practice educator to enable them to assess your understanding of your progress on placement and to use your practice examples to write interim and/or final reports. It may also be submitted to the university as part of the academic assessment to produce your final grade. As such, the evidence portfolio is a critical aspect of your placement development.

Reflective Task 8.1

Can you identify a piece of your work undertaken on placement that you are most proud of?

How does it represent your strengths?

Can you identify where you developed skills within it?

Can you identify any learning needs from it?

The evidence portfolio is considered a good way to enable students to 'show off' their skills and it is student-centred as the student themselves pick the evidence that they would like to use. However, as Edmondson (2014) reminds us, a talent for the practical tasks in placement does not necessarily translate to the ability to identify and compile strong evidence to represent this good practice. Whilst a final report will be the assessor's (your practice educator's) opinion of your work, the evidence portfolio is your time to demonstrate what you have done on placement. It is also an excellent reflective tool for the social work student as it requires you to reflect on which skills you have developed as the placement has progressed. It charts your progress and is a permanent record of your achievement in placement. Doel (2010) argues that, like recording, if you do not provide evidence that it happened, it effectively did not happen. He compares the evidence folder to a photo album, where the pictures (evidence) portray a story of the placement journey.

WHEN TO COMPLETE AN EVIDENCE PORTFOLIO

At the placement learning agreement meeting you should agree when your practice educator requires the evidence portfolio to be handed in to them. Whilst your university may require it on last day of placement, or a set date, the practice educator will require it a short time before to enable them to verify your evidence and write your final report. Whilst this can be reviewed as placement progresses, it is helpful to have a working hand-in date.

However, it is critical to understand that the evidence portfolio is *not* a last-minute, end-of-placement task. Even if you make this mistake on your first placement, I can assure you that you will not do so on your final placement. The most important thing when compiling an evidence folder is to be organised. Like the diving phrase 'equalise early and often', the earlier and more frequently that you review your evidence, the better it will be.

....

POTENTIAL PLACEMENT *PITFALL* Olivia did not start the task of compiling evidence until the last week of placement. At this point she identified that she had not met domain four robustly. She had left herself insufficient time to undertake the unmet placement activities required for her to meet this domain, which would make it impossible for her to pass placement. At this point she had to scramble to meet the domain and undertook a superficial activity by writing a brief letter to housing to advocate for a service user, which met the domain but reduced the effectiveness of the learning from the activity.

POTENTIAL PLACEMENT *OPPORTUNITY* Alexander considered on a monthly basis how his evidence matched his domains, and recognised that he was progressing well, which boosted his self-confidence. It also helped him to identify areas that were not yet met, so that he could plan in supervision activities to ensure that his learning was robust. He identified that he had not met domain 4 robustly. As a result, he was allocated an opportunity to advocate for a service user in a service allocation meeting, where, after critical analysis and reflection on the service user's needs, considering the impact of the structural oppression on their ability to historically engage with the service and their current motivation to change combined with his understanding of the agency context, he was able to secure additional funds to meet their needs by professionally advocating for them within a multi-agency meeting.

....

Whilst both students demonstrated capability within the domain, Alexander's depth of learning enabled him to expand his understanding through reflection from a theoretical, value-base and procedural perspective, as advocated in Chapter 5. Furthermore, discussion with his practice educator enabled him to benefit from collaborative learning.

Matthews et al. (2014) argue that compiling your evidence portfolio requires you to be organised and proactive. It is a lengthy task that requires reflection and planning to achieve. A useful way to view evidence collation – and indeed many universities now have this as part of their structure – is to reflect at the interim stage on the evidence gathered and the domains it meets, and to compile your first piece of evidence per domain at this stage. This will enable you to understand what is asked of you in terms of completing the task and makes the identifying of evidence through the second half of placement easier. It also enables you to identify areas of practice that you may need to explore further in the second half of placement. However, as Matthews et al. gently remind us, do not feel complacent that ongoing evidence folder work negates the need for time to conclude the portfolio at the end of placement, as it will still need pulling together and checking that it includes your best examples for each domain.

Here you should stop and reflect what the 'best' examples are. Are you looking for the assessment where you completed your best critical analysis and recommendations, or are you looking for the one where you learnt the most? It is often considered that providing evidence of development is the 'best' evidence, so consider an assessment that you undertook early in placement and learnt from *and* a later assessment that shows your applied learning. Your practice educator will be an excellent resource in identifying where you have progressed the most and developed a skill or met a domain.

ETHICAL CONSIDERATIONS

You will need to ensure that your evidence portfolio is constructed ethically. Indeed, referring to Fenge et al.'s (2014: 21) 'relevant ... valid ... sufficient ... reliable ... agreed', I would argue that adding 'ethical' to the list further enhances the quality of your evidence.

Looking first at origin, it is important that you are clear about the level of work that you contributed to the evidence. If you observed an assessment being undertaken, but felt that you learnt significantly from this, then it is valid to include, but you *must* identify your observation role, not claim the assessment as your own. In this case, a reflection on your learning from it would be a more appropriate piece of evidence than the assessment you observed, as you did not complete it.

Similarly, co-working is an incredibly valuable and common practice, but ensure that you identify the role you took within the task. Passing work off as your own that is later identified as a colleague's will question your ability to meet domain 1, professionalism. But of course, if you undertook the work independently, also be clear about that: be proud of your achievements.

The second ethical area raised is that of confidentiality. It is incredibly important that you do not place the service user at risk of identification. Mathews et al. (2014) remind us that our protection of a service user's data is their right by law. As such, allocate a false name or an initial for every service user right from the start of your intervention to enable consistency. Avoid long false names as you have to type them repeatedly. Tara and Tim are brilliant names to use. Nevertheless, ensure that the name reflects the service user's cultural identity and gender, and never, ever, change the service user's ethnicity to tick an academic requirement box. Furthermore, use the allocated false name or initial consistently throughout the portfolio, to allow the reader to follow the progress that both yourself and the service user make.

Furthermore, ensure that you delete the service user's identifiable information (e.g. date of birth, address, school or GP surgery) from any paperwork that you choose to use as evidence.

With current technology, this should be a simple deletion process. Never, ever, store evidence on your personal or university electronic device or take paper copies home with you that has service user details on it. The process described above must be undertaken before saving anything to your system.

Some universities will ask that agencies are also anonymised, so rather than using the name of the service, describe them (e.g. 'a substance misuse service'). Similarly, refer to colleagues by their job title rather than by name. However, to complete this task, a confidentiality statement should be included in your evidence portfolio. This should be concise and clear, as Tatiana's shown below.

▰▰▰▰▰▰ Placement Example: Tatiana's Confidentiality Statement ▰▰▰▰▰▰

I have read and abided by my placement agency's confidentiality procedure. Whilst completing this evidence portfolio I have anonymised all service user's names using a chronological alphabetical system (i.e. first service user is Mrs A, second Mrs B etc.), which respects and protects their identity. I have changed all agency names to reflect their service provision, and titled all professionals by their job role.

I have permission from my placement team and practice educator to use their real names, so that university documents can be attached.

Finally, Jones (2014) raises the ethical dilemma of sharing with the service user from the start that as a student you may use the work you undertake with them as an academic reflection, which she rightly states is open and honest, but she also reflects can restrict engagement. However, ethically, the service user should always know from the outset that you may reflect on your work with them, as discussed in Chapter 4.

WHAT EVIDENCE CAN I USE?

Many students struggle with what to use as evidence, and it does have a different emphasis from university to university. Some prefer emphasis on work products, others on reflections. However, generally evidence can be any work product that *you* complete, any reflection that you write, or an item of university proscribed placement paperwork. Some universities ask for a *bundle*, a combination of two or three of these elements as one piece of evidence; other universities will ask for one per piece of evidence per domain. Jones (2014) provides an excellent discussion on the student demonstrating the integration of practical evidence (see 'work products' below) with reflective and theoretical discussion (evidenced in a reflection or supervision discussion) to demonstrate not only the ability to 'do' social work, but also to understand the 'why' of social work intervention. Fenge et al. (2014: 21) reflect, instead, that it is the *quality* of evidence that is critical, and recommend that you ask of each piece of evidence 'Is it ... relevant ... valid ...

sufficient ... reliable ... agreed?'. Both are valid perspectives and merit thought before you begin evidence collation. As you compile your evidence consider the purpose of the document, what is it showing and which skill(s) will it demonstrate. On the document, highlight a specific section if that is the relevant part to the domain, or provide a brief description of how you feel it meets the domain.

Evidence can be divided into work products and placement documents. Work products can include:

Case recording: Ensure they are anonymised and relevant. Only include the necessary record, as your professionalism will be questioned if you provide unnecessary records. They often match to intervention and skills (PCF7) or contexts and organisations (PCF8).

Documents: Any agency documents that you complete can be evidence, for example assessments, support or care plans, placement forms, referral forms to other agencies. Ensure that all forms that you use have personal details redacted. They may meet intervention and skills (PCF7) and professionalism (PCF1) – if in timescale. A critically analytical assessment may meet critical reflection (PCF6).

Correspondence: Letters, emails and case recording of telephone calls can be included if they clearly meet a domain. Ask yourself what is this demonstrating to ensure relevance, but often meets rights and justice (PCF4) if they advocate or represent.

However, these should be supplemented with university proscribed placement documents, including:

Feedback: A service user's perspective can often be very different from a colleague's feedback, so ensure that both are heard. This is discussed further in Chapters 3 and 4. Feedback can meet professionalism (PCF1), values and ethics (PCF2) or intervention and skills (PCF7).

Supervision: All supervision should be recorded and agreed. The minutes should demonstrate the work that you have undertaken, so meet domain 1 professionalism (PCF1), intervention and skills (PCF7), context and organisations (PCF8) and professional leadership (PCF9), but also discuss a wide variety of topics including values (PCF2), diversity (PCF3), social work theory (PCF5), and be reflective (PCF6). They are a rich source of evidence, but do ensure that you highlight the section that you wish to match the nominated domain and that they are anonymised.

Case summaries: Providing a summary of work undertaken by yourself with each service user makes excellent evidence for domain 7. Edmondson (2014) suggests using the headings *referral, background, assessment, plan, intervention* and *summary of practice* to explore your practice. You can enhance your learning and further demonstrate your capability by also implementing a theoretical basis (PCF5) for your work and reflecting (PCF6) on your practice (PCF7), values (PCF2), or the context of the intervention (PCF8).

Reflections: As discussed in Chapter 6, this should cover a variety of issues and perspectives. This means that across your reflections they can meet each and every domain, dependent on the topic.

Reflective Task 8.2

Look back at the reflections from Chapter 6, which domains do you feel each one meets? First list all the domains you feel the reflection meets, then identify which domain it best meets.

> *Placement learning application (PLA) form*: This can demonstrate professionalism (PCF1) if it is done in the required timescale as it shows note-taking and organisational skills.
>
> *Direct observations*: As discussed in Chapters 2 and 3, you are required to be observed a minimum of three times, which will demonstrate your planning and practice professionalism (PCF1) and intervention and skills (PCF7), but will also provide an opportunity for observer feedback on your ability to value a service user (PCF2), or represent the service (PCF8).
>
> *Interim report*: I strongly advise against using this as it is a repetition of your first evidence match.
>
> *Academic assignment*: As discussed in Chapter 9, there are a range of assignments set for social work students on placement, but the commonality between them is a reflective perspective on your practice. Some universities actively encourage one piece of evidence to be identified for each domain for the evidence portfolio, while others discourage it completely.

Irrespective of the evidence you choose, or are asked, to use, make sure you identify where and how you feel that your evidence meets the domain. You may know that paragraph four of a three-page supervision minutes is the relevant section, but unless you indicate this, the practice educator or tutor will not be aware of it. Also, make sure that the evidence is clear that it meets a domain. Do not assume that because you know that meeting someone who misuses substances triggered a personal and professional value discussion with a colleague, that a case record of the visit demonstrates this.

POTENTIAL PLACEMENT *PITFALL* Leah's evidence was vague, and her practice educator could not see how she felt the evidence demonstrated the domain. She was asked to resubmit her evidence folder with explanations of the links.

POTENTIAL PLACEMENT *OPPORTUNITY* James' evidence was clear and his practice educator was able to write a robust and in-depth final report, which encouraged his prospective second placement practice educator to accept him in a complex team.

As you identify evidence during your placement, check with your practice educator that they feel that your proposed evidence is relevant. Lomax and Jones (2014) recommend that evidence identification is not a solo task, instead that working with your practice educator will ensure that it meets their expectations of evidence. They may even have better examples that you have not thought could be appropriate. Use this as another learning opportunity: discuss with your practice educator how you developed during a piece of work, and reflect on their responses.

What new ideas come from this discussion, does it lead to exploration of different theories or skill development?

HOW TO COMPLETE YOUR EVIDENCE PORTFOLIO

In order to ensure that your evidence is clear and matches well with the evidence criteria, there are two phases to completing a successful evidence portfolio: identify the work that you have undertaken on placement; and what criteria it can meet. This task can be broken into three further subsections (Table 8.1 shows Henrietta's evidence portfolio as an example):

1   To begin to identify evidence, you need to have a clear outline of the work you have undertaken whilst on placement, so that you can see holistically the range of work that you should draw on, as sometimes you may forget or disregard a good piece of work from early on in placement. Indeed, some universities ask for a 'work undertaken' list to be provided. This list should be written as your placement progresses. Update your workload on each service user weekly in an anonymised list to ensure you do not forget earlier interventions.
2   Once you have a clear idea of the work that you have undertaken, you can start to identify the evidence from your work. *Using* the evidence work products and university placement documents discussed earlier in the chapter, identify what evidence you have from each piece of work.
3   Once you have a clear list of potential evidence you can start to match the evidence to the required criteria it could meet. If we look at Henrietta's evidence (Table 8.1) from working with Family A and match it to PCF domains (HCPC, 2018), then we will see that there is a deep breadth of work that can be used. An example of SOPs (HCPC, 2015) met is also provided to demonstrate that it can be applied to a variety of criteria.

Table 8.1   Example of Henrietta's evidence-domain matching

Work undertaken, family A	Evidence produced	PCF domain match	SOP match
Initial assessment of family	Assessment of child BA	6: Critical analysis 7: Intervention and skills	Be able to practice as an autonomous professional, exercising their own professional judgement. Understand the need to establish and maintain a safe practice environment.
Individual support plan	Support plan for CA	7: Intervention and skills	Be able to draw on appropriate knowledge and skills to inform practice.
Co-wrote conference report	Conference report	6: Critical analysis 7: Intervention and skills	Be able to practise safely and effectively within the scope of their practice.

(Continued)

Table 8.1   (Continued)

Work undertaken, family A	Evidence produced	PCF domain match	SOP match
Attended and participated in conference	Conference minutes Reflection 4: How agencies interact Direct observation 2	1: Professionalism 6: Critical analysis 7: Intervention and skills 8: Contexts and organisations	Be able to practice within legal and ethical boundaries of their profession. Be able to work appropriately with others.
Weekly support visits	Case recording Supervision notes Service user feedback	1: Professionalism 6: Critical analysis 7: Intervention and skills	Understand importance of and be able to maintain confidentiality. Be able to maintain records appropriately.
Advocated for after school club provision funding	Letter	4: Rights and justice	Be able to communicate effectively.
Direct work with child DA	Case recording Reflection 6: DA's cultural identity as a mixed-race step child to white parents	2: Values and ethics 3: Diversity 7: Intervention and skills 9: Professional leadership	Be aware of the impact of culture, equality and diversity on practice. Be able to practise in a non-discriminatory manner.
Home visit	Reflection 9: Impact of domestic abuse on children	2: Values and ethics 5: Knowledge 6: Critical analysis	Be able to reflect on and review practice. Understand the key concepts of the knowledge base relevant to their profession.

You can see from this that each piece of evidence may meet more than one domain. For example, domain 1 could have been included in every single example as they all demonstrate Henrietta's professionalism in different ways. The key element here is not to over-identify domains, pick only the strongest domains the evidence meets. Repeat this activity for the work you have undertaken with each service user, providing yourself with a breadth of evidence to pull on. But also consider non-service user specific work that you have undertaken, for example facilitating a group, researching a topic to present to a team meeting, or attending a training. All provide rich opportunities for learning and skill development.

Identify the right evidence for each domain

Once you have a clear picture of the evidence that you have available, and the potential domains that it could meet, you need to move to the second phase of evidence folder creation: identifying the right evidence for the right domain.

At this stage, I would introduce to you a simple grid (Table 8.2) that can be very effective to use as an ongoing evidence gathering tool. You can replace the PCF domains with your own criteria as required.

Table 8.2 PCF evidence grid

Domain	Evidence 1	Evidence 1	Evidence 1
Professionalism			
Values and ethics			
Diversity			
Rights and justice			
Knowledge			
Critical reflection			
Intervention and skills			
Contexts and organisations			
Professional leadership			

The principle of this grid is that you aim to have your best three (although different universities may ask for different numbers) pieces of evidence by the end of placement. The knack is to use your list of evidence–domain matches (as Table 8.1) and fill in the grid piece of evidence by piece of evidence, replacing stronger evidence as you progress. I feel that it is like a jigsaw, you move your pieces of evidence round until you get the optimum combination. Cut and paste on a computer is excellent for this task, as it enables you to move evidence round efficiently. You can even save different versions as you progress.

Always ensure that you demonstrate both the breadth of work that you undertook, but also the breadth of service users with whom you worked. From this you should be able to see how planning combined with a holistic viewing of your work can ensure that you meet all of your domains effectively in your evidence portfolio (see Table 8.3).

Table 8.3 Completed evidence grid

Domain	Evidence 1	Evidence 2	Evidence 3
Professionalism	Conference minutes family A	Supervision notes on family B – discussed integrity	Direct observation 3
Values and ethics	Service user feedback family B	Direct observation 1	Reflection 9: impact of domestic abuse on children
Diversity	Reflection 1: my first observed home visit and how I felt about poverty	Reflection 6: DA's cultural identity as a mixed-race step child to white parents	Duty work case recording: support young person who wanted to leave home
Rights and justice	Advocacy letter child AA Referral to substance misuse service, family B	Case recording: t/c re Mr D's benefit application Reflection 7: service criteria, family C	Case recording: Direct work with child DA to promote self-esteem
Knowledge	Training certificate Reflection 3: what I learnt at training	Reflection 5: how I implemented task-centred intervention with family B	Reflection 9: impact of domestic abuse on children
Critical reflection	Assessment of child BA	Reflection 4: how agencies interact Reflection 7: service criteria, family C	Reflection 9: Impact of domestic abuse on children
Intervention and skills	Assessment of child BA Support plan for CA	Assessment of child GB Conference report and minutes family A	Co-led parenting group: planning sheet and reflection Direct work with child FD: case notes
Contexts and organisations	Attend regular team meetings Completed induction programme	Reflection 4: how agencies interact Reflection 7: service criteria, family C	Conference report and minutes family A Minutes from Early Years meeting I chaired family B
Professional leadership	Co-led parenting group: planning sheet and reflection	Team meeting minutes of presenting information (appropriate CAMHS referrals)	Minutes from Early Years meeting I chaired family D

POTENTIAL PLACEMENT *PITFALL* Olivia was short of time compiling her evidence portfolio, so thought of three excellent pieces of practice that she had undertaken on placement: an assessment, a home visit on which she was observed, and a meeting she participated in. For each one she anonymised and copied the relevant paperwork (the assessment, the case recording and direct observation sheet, and the meeting minutes) and found a relevant reflection that linked to each piece of work. She put these in each domain and used them to demonstrate her practice.

When her final report came out, she was deeply disappointed that it did not represent the breadth of excellent work that she had undertaken in her final placement.

POTENTIAL PLACEMENT *OPPORTUNITY* Henrietta provided a breadth of evidence in her portfolio, and she was delighted with her final report, which demonstrated her breadth of work and learning on placement.

Olivia did not value the evidence matching exercise and did not feel that it added value to her placement outcome, but was disappointed in the outcome in her final report. She reflected that *you only get out what you put in* and she vowed to undertake evidence gathering and matching earlier in her second placement.

Reflective Task 8.3

Using the grid in Table 8.2, reflect on your placement so far (or think back to your volunteering experience), and think of one example of your practice for every domain.

Some domains will be harder for others, so spend time undertaking this task.

If you are unable to find a different example, consider if this means that you need to talk to your practice educator about enhancing your learning opportunities.

Having tried it once, doing it three times for placement should be easier.

PLACEMENT PERSPECTIVE 8.2

Student's thoughts on compiling the evidence portfolio

Identifying what you are capable of for the PCF is confusing at first. I found it helpful to discuss the work I had been doing in supervisions. My practice educator helped me build the correlation between theory and legislation to my practice. I also found that doing the weekly reflections broadened my knowledge of my practice and developed my personal intuition, which enabled me to self-analyse and begin to reflect 'in' practice. The more I understood about my practice, the more confidence I became as I was able to fully understand the nature of the interventions and match them to the PCF domains.

I found that writing things down as soon as they happened helped me to include the correct information. Then in my study time I looked through my activities and chose the strongest to use as my evidence. I found it helpful to speak to my practice educator about areas that I found were weak, and they arranged for me to be involved in activities that allowed me to strengthen my evidence. An example of this was for domain 9: Leadership, it was arranged that I chaired a meeting.

Be organised, use your supervisions and study time, and ask for help!

Stacey Mallinder, BA Social Work

CHAPTER SUMMARY

In conclusion, your evidence folder should demonstrate the breadth of work that you have undertaken in placement: this is your opportunity to exhibit your achievements. The final report may be written by your practice educator, but is based on your evidence folder, so invest time to make it reflect your accomplishments. To fully enhance your learning from placement, reflect on your learning activities, as retrospective learning – or *reflection on action* as Schon (1983) would label it – is beneficial as you take advantage of a holistic overview of the placement. Furthermore, Matthews et al. (2014) recommend that as you complete your evidence portfolio, you should consider your learning needs for your future placement or first qualified role.

CHAPTER CHECKLIST

In order to maximise your learning from your evidence compilation:

- ✔ begin to compile your evidence portfolio early in placement, and see it as an ongoing task
- ✔ demonstrate your breadth of work undertaken on your placement
- ✔ use the recommended evidence grid system to avoid excessive repetition.

████████████ **Further reading** ████████████

Chapter 2 'Evidencing your capability using the professional capability framework', in Fenge, L., Howe, K., Hughes, M. and Thomas, G. (2014) *The Social Work Portfolio: A Student's Guide to Evidencing your Practice*. Maidenhead: Open University Press.

Chapter 5 'Completing your portfolio', in Jones, S. (2015) *Social Work Practice Placements*. London: SAGE.

Chapter 7 'Processes and practicalities', in Matthews, I., Simpson, D. and Crawford, K. (2014) *Your Social Work Practice Placement: From Start to Finish*. London: SAGE.

9

WRITING YOUR PLACEMENT ASSIGNMENT

This chapter will provide generic advice on placement assignment writing, but also acknowledge variety across university placement assignments. It will look at the core themes that ask the student to write an assignment based on the ability to match an intervention to specified criteria; an assignment that asks the student to provide a case study that analyses theories and skills used; and an assignment that demands reflection on learning from placement. The style of assignment will vary, but the common theme will be an expectation for a more reflective style of writing. Therefore, this chapter will be usefully read in conjunction with Chapter 6. It will consider how to identify future learning needs and include them in assignment.

═══════════════ **PLACEMENT PERSPECTIVE 9.1** ═══════════════

Tutor's perspective on placement assignments

For many students, the final practice assignment represents the culmination of placement. It is usually the final piece of assessed work and many marks can be at stake. In the case of final qualifying placements, degree classifications may depend on a good result. With so much hinging on one assignment, it is not surprising that students may be anxious, as well as having significant emotional investment in the assignment.

Students tend to select the most complex practice learning opportunity they have worked with as their focus and part of the reason for this might be in order to process the events. This may have some advantages because there should be ample

scope to link in reflection, legislation, policy and theory, which will all attract higher marks. However, just because a piece of practice has not been 'perfect' should not prevent it from being a good focus to choose. There can be much to gain from analysing practice that has not gone entirely as expected or where problems have occurred. Indeed, sometimes it makes a better assignment as it enables you to reflect on your practice well. What is essential, whether the work has gone to plan or not, is that the student draws out what they have learned and what can be taken forward into future practice situations.

As someone who has marked many practice assignments, I would always advise against

(Continued)

telling too much of a story. There should be enough detail to convey what has happened but unnecessary details, which are not strictly relevant, can be left out. Students should make sure there are no identifying factors that could breach confidentiality. In a complex piece of work, it might be best to focus on a particular episode or event – that way the exploration of issues in sufficient depth is manageable. It may seem obvious, but students should also make sure that they address the module learning outcomes and familiarise themselves with any advice given to them by their university regarding the assignment. Remember that this may vary between first and second placement opportunities.

The best practice assignments tend to include a thorough discussion of ethical and value considerations. Descriptions of practice that centrally place the promotion of service users' rights and responsibilities in a legislative and policy context tend to achieve high marks, as does evaluative and analytical discussion. It is very important to be aware of the language used within the work and to explain any professional jargon or terms.

Finally, I would advocate selecting a range of reading, researching and background sources that will inform your understanding of the situation both during your practice and at time of writing your assignment. It is important to remember that this is an assignment about practice, and practice should be central, but it is also vital to show how relevant knowledge has an influence, particularly when drawing out learning.

Mary Harrison, Senior Lecturer in Social Work

ASSIGNMENT WRITING SKILLS

By the time you are on placement, you will have written a variety of other assignments. Musson (2011: 2) argues that 'effort + time + application of skills = work of quality'. He makes a valid point. If you want to produce a good quality assignment you will need to allocate time to plan, read, plan, write, review, read, write and submit. Gill and Medd (2015) recommend, as have many other authors, the use of a timetable to plan what you need to do when. Given that you will have to juggle placement, personal commitments (family, job etc.) and other academic work, this is no less true on placement. However, they warn of debilitating avoidance through timetable and to-do list creation.

There are some core tips that I would recommend when writing any assignment. Be aware of other assignment hand-in dates and plan to allow time to produce your best work for each piece of work. Ensure that you understand what is being asked of you, the title, the marking criteria against which you will be marked, and word count. Musson (2011) advocates a clear understanding of the assignment title and emphasises understanding the verb in the assignment title to ensure that your response is relevant. For example, if the assignment asks you to compare and contrast your skills at beginning and end within an assessment, but you only reflect on one assessment, you will not have responded to the assignment brief. Ensure that you know the hand-in date and hand-in procedure, which IT system it must be uploaded on or office handed in to. Such details will all be in your module handbook, but if in doubt, ask your module leader to ensure that you have understood correctly.

Furthermore, the marker will look for depth of knowledge. For example, do not just put 'Children Act 1989', state the section that you are referring to. Use the social work framework you have to support your discussion, do not just name the Code of Ethics for Social Workers, paraphrase its content to show you have read it and reference it correctly with author, page and year. In order to demonstrate professional writing, adopt a grammatically correct style, good spelling and avoid the use of slang within assignments. Do not use acronyms without first defining them, and avoid contractions such as 'don't'.

POTENTIAL PLACEMENT *PITFALL* Jakub was enjoying placement so much that he forgot he needed to provide a placement assignment. It was only when he saw on Facebook others celebrating that they had handed in that he realised he needed to write it. He pulled an 'all-nighter' between placement days and was able to hand in on time. However, he was disappointed with his grade. When he re-read the assignment he could see errors and recognised the feedback that it did not reflect his learning on placement.

POTENTIAL PLACEMENT *OPPORTUNITY* Nadja was enjoying placement as much a Jakub, but ensured from start of placement that she had assignment dates in her diary so that she could plan and write her assignment in good time. She was able to write a placement assignment that reflected her learning on placement and was academically solid. She gained a grade that she was delighted with.

Bottomley et al. (2018: 20) note that *being realistic* is key to successful assignment writing. They advocate a balanced yet reasonable mix of study and attention to non-academic tasks. This is good advice. On placement you will need to balance placement work, academic work, personal work or family commitments with time for yourself. Exercise and relaxation can be as important a part of the assignment writing strategy as the reading of books and writing the assignment itself, as they contribute heavily to your emotional wellbeing. Plan ten minute breaks into every hour study time or pre-book an exercise class, but look after yourself.

A good way to enhance your academic profile is to refer back to your feedback from previous assignments. Stogdon and Kiteley (2010) support its value to enhance your writing style. If you regularly get feedback that you need to develop your referencing or address your assignment structure, seek support with it. Every university has an excellent resource pool of e-learning, podcasts, books, and/or group or individual tutorials that are there to support your development, so use them. Markers spend time constructing your feedback so that you can improve your next assignment by learning from the advice, so take advantage of it.

Reflective Task 9.1

Think back to feedback on previous assignments. Can you identify themes of feedback that you need to address to enhance your assignment writing skills?

Time spent preparing your assignment is time well spent. Use your module handbook reading list: I can promise you that your module leader has checked out the most relevant books to access for you; do not just search online and then use an unknown (and sometimes irrelevant or misleading) source because you cannot get into the university library. Read from a range of sources, because academic marking will look for breadth of researching. Using recommended books, looking at relevant journal articles, and re-reading lecture notes and listening to lecture recordings will all enhance your understanding of the topic, and demonstrate academic commitment.

By this point you will start to have a feel for what you want to write about. Construct an assignment plan that sets out an introduction, three core themes to discuss, and a conclusion. Identify key areas to discuss within each core theme. If you are feeling overwhelmed by an assignment, this is a good way to break it down into more achievable tasks. Nevertheless, do make sure that there is a flow between the different themes so that you develop an argument. Send your assignment plan to the module leader or your tutor (depending on the support your university offers), allowing plenty of time for them to respond and you to still have time to write your assignment.

Once you have completed your first full draft of the assignment, you then need to spend some time on attention to detail, which always enhances your grade. By proofreading it after some separation (at least 24 hours) you will see spelling and grammar mistakes and be able to identify where the flow and structure confuses the reader. Musson (2011) reminds us of the importance of good sentence construction and avoidance of slang in assignments. Ensure that your academic referencing is correct. Your university will have a set referencing strategy and e-learning on it, so use the resources available to ensure that you are able to write to maximise your grade. Stogdon and Kiteley (2010) summarise referencing as recording all sources you use, and ensuring that it is clear when and how you have used their work. Smale and Fowlie (2015) remind you that copying some one else's ideas or words without referencing acknowledgement is plagiarism. In a profession where honesty and integrity are key social work values, one can see the importance of good quality referencing.

Ten Top Tips for Writing an Assignment

1 Know and understand your assignment title.
2 Plan your time carefully, as you may have a number of deadlines at a similar time.
3 Understand your assignment marking criteria so that you understand what is expected of you
4 Utilise your module reading list – it has the most relevant books for the assignment listed in it.
5 Write an assignment plan, and ask the relevant tutor or module leader to comment on its appropriateness.
6 Concentrate on a small number of themes in greater depth, rather than lots of themes in no depth.
7 Read the feedback from other assignments and apply learning to enhance this assignment.
8 Do not listen to social media gossip on the correct answer: check with your module leader when in doubt.
9 Allow time to proofread your assignment.
10 Ensure that your referencing is undertaken correctly.

Hopefully you will have developed strong assignment writing strategies by the time you go on placement. A placement-based assignment is likely to be a little different from some other assignments you will be asked to write whilst on your course as it requires reflecting on your work, so will be written in the first person ('I'). Do not see placement as separated from university teaching. The phrase *applying theory to practice* is often used, and is most useful here. The placement assignment is an opportunity to demonstrate integrated learning and make those links, as we now go on to discuss.

DIFFERENT COURSES, DIFFERENT ACADEMIC ASSIGNMENTS

As referred to earlier in the book, your module handbook or placement handbook will contain the specifics in relation to your course. This book should not replace your understanding of your university's academic requirements but supplement them. Generally, they fall into three key themes of assignments, which we will consider in turn:

- an assignment based on the ability to match an intervention to a number of domains
- an assignment that asks the student to provide a case study that analyses theories and skills used
- an assignment that demands reflection on learning from placement.

Domain-related assignments

When your placement assignment asks you to match an experience or intervention you have undertaken to a domain or set criteria, you will need to think about how you match these. Chapter 8 explains a good process to do this for an evidence folder, and the same principles can be followed in an assignment. Usually the university will ask that these are different examples to the evidence grid discussed in that chapter, but check their expectation of you. You do not want to self-plagiarise, but neither do you want to undertake unnecessary work.

Earlier we suggested that an assignment has an introduction, three key themes, and a conclusion. Domain-related assignments break that mould: if you have nine domains, there will be nine themes, and obviously fewer words per theme to use.

Assignment Plan 9.1

Introduction: Briefly set out that this will cover each of the PCF domains, utilising a range of intervention examples, supported where appropriate with theoretical perspective

Domain 1: Example of how you were professional, the skills your learnt and support it with theory.

Domain 2: Example of when your values were challenged and support it with theory.

Domain 3: Example of how you challenged a diversity issue, the skills your learnt and support it with theory.

(Continued)

Domain 4: Example of you advocating for a service user, the skills your learnt and support it with theory.

Domain 5: Example of how you have applied theory to an intervention to inform your practice.

Domain 6: Example of how you reflected on your practice and what you have learnt from it.

Domain 7: Example of an intervention, the skills your learnt and support it with theory.

Domain 8: Example of inter-professional working, the skills your learnt and support it with theory.

Domain 9: Example of leading a group or sharing information, the skills your learnt and support it with theory.

Conclusion: What skills you have learnt whilst on placement.

You will need to describe clearly and concisely the intervention you will refer to. It is a difficult and crucial skill to write concisely, to include enough information so that the reader knows the important and relevant information. This will be followed by critical analysis of the skill used, supported academically with relevant theory. If your assignment question asks you to reflect on a choice of three domains, for example, then you will be able to apply this pattern but in more depth.

....

POTENTIAL PLACEMENT *PITFALL* Penny had a wide range of excellent learning opportunities, so had a breadth of intervention examples to provide in her placement assignment. She began writing freely, but by domain 4 (of 9) had used the total word limit for the assignment. She wanted to ensure that the marker understood all the nuances of her work so submitted the first four domains only, but by being unable to address all nine domains she did not meet the assignment brief and received a low grade.

POTENTIAL PLACEMENT *OPPORTUNITY* Petra had a wide range of excellent learning opportunities, so had a breadth of intervention examples to provide in her placement assignment. Before she began writing she calculated the words she could allocate to each domain (word limit divided by domains) and saw each domain as a mini-reflection where she described the intervention, skill developed and provided an academic reference. She was able to address the assignment requirements and was delighted with her grade.

....

Often students struggle to fit everything in to such a small word limit, so stop for an hour and write a 300-word summary of a piece of work you have undertaken, the skills developed, and put in an academic reference. Hard isn't it? You will need to accept that you cannot provide the breadth of discussion that you can luxuriate in in other assignments. Sometimes that is the hardest part of this style of placement assignment, so be prepared to argue with yourself!

Case study assignment

Many universities ask the student to provide a case study or case summary of a piece of work they have undertaken, sometimes called a critical analysis of practice (CAP). The first important step in this style of placement assignment is the choice of intervention. You need to identify it by interim stage in your placement to enable you to have enough time to write the assignment, but often the more complex works comes in the second half of placement. But be bold. Do not keep changing your mind as more work is allocated, as it will confuse you and the assignment. Furthermore, choose a piece of work that is sufficiently complex to highlight your skills and knowledge, but that is time limited so that you do not spend most of your words saying 'and then this happened'. I would advise concentrating your assignment on one event within your intervention (a home visit, assessment, interprofessional meeting etc.). This will enable you to provide depth of discussion on one piece of work, rather than spreading yourself too thinly covering a wide range of issues.

Earlier I suggested using a plan of introduction, three themes, conclusion, and this assignment lends itself to this model. Choose three areas that you want to look at to support your intervention. That could be a specific intervention skill, a value or ethical issue, a problem you encountered and overcame.

Assignment Plan 9.2

Introduction: Set out the intervention that you will focus on, the theory that you will apply to your practice, and the reflections that you will make on your practice.

Definition: Briefly describe your intervention.

Theme One – Values: Describe an ethical dilemma that challenged your values within the intervention, critically explore different perspectives in relation to the dilemma, discuss the values and theory behind your dilemma, and conclude with your learning from this incident.

Theme Two – Application of theory to practice: Describe in a little more detail the intervention and explain the theoretical basis that you worked within. Ensure that you integrate the theory and the practice rather than describing in one paragraph and theorising in the next. Conclude with your learning from this theory.

Theme Three – Professionalism through supervision: Describe how you used supervision to support your development of and reflection on your skills and knowledge and understanding of the policies and procedures. Apply theoretical perspective and learning on how to best use supervision.

Conclusion: Summarise your learning from the case study, and identify any future learning needs that will inform your next placement or first qualified job.

The important task in this style of placement assignment is the depth of discussion. Cover fewer themes in more depth to enhance your grade.

Reflective Task 9.2

Think of a recent intervention (e.g. home visit) you have undertaken. First, list *all* the themes raised within that piece of work: the skills you used, the knowledge you drew on, the service user's perspective, the

(Continued)

agency perspective, legislation used, your personal or professional values, any discrimination you observed, the context of the service, the context of the service user's needs and so on.

Next, identify the three most significant themes. Do not think too hard, just identify them quite quickly.

Start to reflect on why you chose those three themes, what interested you about them? What are the key issues within the theme?

You now have the basis for your assignment plan.

....

Reflection-on-learning assignment

This is the same as the previous assignment, but turned on its head. Instead of thinking of the intervention first and identifying learning from the work, you identify your learning from placement and then use an intervention to evidence it. Sometimes it is called a 'learning highlight'. Your university may provide specific areas it requires to reflect upon, for example choose from how you have developed your professionalism, interprofessional working, values or self-awareness, or just name one area. As ever, ensure that you read the assignment question carefully.

If you have a choice, consider which area your placement has provided the greatest learning opportunities for you in. There is no point in writing on interprofessional working if you have had limited opportunities in that area. Give yourself the best chance to write a good assignment.

.... ┌──────────────────────┐
      │ **Reflective Task 9.3** │ ....
      └──────────────────────┘

Identify what you have learnt on placement so far in relation to professionalism and the skills you feel you still need to develop.

Can you provide an example to support each item on your lists?

This is your assignment plan.

....

In this assignment you need to be reflective first and foremost. Think back to your self-assessment in Chapter 1. I asked you not to be too self-critical, but neither to be full of yourself. The same applies here. The marker will look for a balanced reflection on both your skills and your areas for development.

Break the skill into three themes; in professionalism that might be time management skills, working in a person-centred manner and case-note recording skills. Within each theme you should provide the theory of the theme, an example of your practice, your learning from the work, and identify any learning needs in that theme. It is a relatively formulaic assignment, but undertaken well is very effective.

━━━━━━━━━ **Assignment Plan 9.3** ━━━━━━━━━

Introduction: Clearly state the skill (professionalism in this example) you intend to reflect upon, and state that you will explore it on a theoretical basis and reflect upon your skill development within it, supported by examples of your practice.

Definition: Briefly define professionalism. Use a relevant social work definition.

Theme One: Define time management skills, discuss the theoretical perspective, and apply to your practice by using an example of your work. Reflect on your skill development and learning needs.

Theme Two: Define person-centred practice, and repeat as above.

Theme Three: Define case-note management, and repeat as above.

Conclusion: Summarise the skill, your examples of work and learning from your experience. Conclude with your identified learning needs.

CRITICAL ANALYSIS

The link between all three types of placement assignment is the request for critical analysis. Your perspective, which should look at a number of different sides within one discussion, should be supported with academic reasoning: an *evidence-based rationale* (Bottomley et al., 2018: 54). Stogdon and Kiteley (2010) strongly advocate against simply paraphrasing from textbooks, recommending instead that you ensure that you demonstrate your own views within your interpretation of said textbook.

Chapter 6 explores how to write reflectively, and you should read that chapter in conjunction with this one when writing a placement assignment. But remember not to over-describe the event, as the reflection and critical analysis are the important aspect of the assignment.

APPLYING THEORY TO PRACTICE

In order to be able to undertake an intervention effectively, as a social work student you need to understand why you are undertaking the intervention, and the strategies that you are drawing on. Initially, you are likely to have used your natural skills, imitated your practice educator and colleagues, and focused on developing your skills, which you should explore the theoretical basis of in supervision with your practice educator. However, as you progress through placement, you need to become more proactive of your application of your knowledge of social work theory to understand the mechanisms that ensure effective interventions. This link of theory to practice is critical to your development as a social worker. Maclean and Harrison (2015) argue that theory helps you to understand a situation, explain why decisions are made and understand outcomes. It contributes to your effective professionalism.

Many students are able to describe the intervention and discuss the theory, but to enhance your understanding, practice and academic grade further, you to need to integrate the two.

To integrate theory and practice you need, in the same paragraph, to describe the intervention and outline the theory you used.

Reflective Task 9.4

Think about an intervention you have undertaken in your placement recently. Focus on one small element, perhaps how you introduced yourself or how you sought the service user's wishes and feelings. Describe it briefly (100–200 words).

Next, consider the theory that you used. Explain the theory (200–400 words).

Finally, re-read both elements and start to intertwine the two.

Students often struggle to *name* a theory, thinking of attachment or person-centred theory, when actually, the assignment needs to refer to the relevant books on subject. Applying theory to practice can simply mean, where you discuss communication, refer to social work communication books, when you discuss values, refer to values books and so on. Keeping this simple but integrated *throughout* your assignment is the key for a placement assignment. Nevertheless, some assignments benefit from a theme running throughout; for example, you might use Kolb's (1984) experiential learning cycle to build your discussion within. Similarly, the ASPIRE model – assessment, planning, intervention, review, evaluation – (Sutton, 1994) provides you with a framework that enables you to reflect on the different stages of your work with a service user. But do not let that be your only theory, still apply relevant references from books and journals throughout.

Authors such as Maclean and Harrison (2015) provide a summary of theories as a starting point for this task. Use it to identify the theory, but always read beyond that into more detailed discussions once you have determined the most appropriate one. Do not be afraid that you have used more than one theory in an intervention. Social work is often a hybrid of drawing on a range of theories that enables the social worker to understand a complex situation.

Reflective Task 9.4 (continued)

Now consider, is there a values issue or ethical debate in the example above? Can you add this into it (200–300 words)? Does this need a theoretical basis to support your discussion (100 words)?

What is the legislative basis for your work (100 words)?

You are now layering the first section of your assignment and ensuring that you are applying theory to practice. Continue this with the next element of your practice and you will be well underway with your placement assignment.

FUTURE LEARNING NEEDS

Many placement assignments will require the student to look at their future learning needs in their next placement or ASYE to conclude. Refer back to your own learning needs identified in Reflective Task 1.2, and reflect upon what you have learnt whilst on placement and identify what you still need to learn in that area. However, one must recognise that you may have had other learning needs, not identified until part way through placement, or that it is only through developing one skill that a future skill is identified for future development. Completing Reflective Task 9.5 will be very helpful in ensuring that you are robust in your reflection on this area.

Reflective Task 9.5

Complete Table 9.1 to help you to identify your future learning needs.

Table 9.1   Identifying future learning needs

Identified learning need	Learning through placement	Ongoing learning needs

Finally, as a marker, I use the phrase 'adding value'. What I mean by that is, does every discussion add to the final grade? A discussion on attachment theory in relation to the service user's need may be excellent, but if the question is reflect on your understanding of the context of the placement, the attachment discussion does not add value to your grade. Make sure all your discussions are relevant to the assignment and module learning outcomes.

■■■■■ PLACEMENT PERSPECTIVE 9.2 ■■■■■

Student Perspective

At the start of the placement I ensured that I organised my time, for example knowing when all deadlines were due and pre-scheduling study days. I set myself tasks for each study

(Continued)

day, and spoke to my practice educator for suggestions. I would recommend that you work out when you study most effectively. I quickly realised that placement was challenging and that by evenings I was too tired to concentrate effectively, so dedicated time in the mornings to study. I also tried not to study at the weekends in order to feel refreshed for placement, but recognised that I needed to as the due date drew closer.

I approached the reflective assignment by selecting an experience that I encountered where I felt I had made a positive impact, as I wanted to self-evaluate my strengths and key skills with a view to identifying areas that I could further develop. I linked the assignment structure to a theoretical model, which allowed me to structure the assignment into a logical order and guided me to explore and reflect upon specific areas. I reflected on each stage of my involvement, which allowed me to break down the case and to identify key areas where I applied theory and knowledge.

Adele Clark, MA Social Work Student

CHAPTER SUMMARY

The academic placement assignment often provides your grade for your placement, so is a critical element of the social work course. It can be easy to lose sight of its importance whilst out on placement, so ensure that you are allocating time to its construction in the second half of your placement. All normal academic advice applies, but the placement assignment also demands that you are critically reflective on your practice and skill development, whilst applying theory to your practice. Finally, see the placement assignment as an opportunity to learn from your practice and enhance your understanding of your practice.

CHAPTER CHECKLIST

In order to enhance your placement assignment academic grade and maximise your understanding of theory:

✔ be organised; ensure that you understand the assignment, know when it is due and write it in good time
✔ integrate your application of theory to your practice throughout your assignment
✔ critically reflect on your social work skills throughout and provide future learning needs.

■■■■■ Further reading ■■■■■

Chapter 4 'Critical thinking in studying for your social work degree', in Bottomley, J., Cartney, P. and Pryjmachuk, S. (2018) *Studying for your Social Work Degree*. St Albans: Critical Publishing.
Maclean, S. and Harrison, R. (2015) *A Straightforward Guide to Theory for Social Work Students*. Lichfield: Kirwin Maclean Associates.

10

CONCLUSION

It is hoped that this book has supported you to navigate a social work placement success-fully. The philosophy of the book has been to ask you to engage with learning opportunities enthusiastically, both in order to get that all-important pass in placement and, far more importantly, to maximise your development as a social work student. The philosophy of the book throughout has been twofold. First, that the more you put into placement, the more you will get out of placement. A learning opportunity is only that: an opportunity. You have to be motivated and committed to your own learning to in order to take advantage of that learning opportunity. By reflecting on your strengths and developing your skills in all areas of placement, you have enhanced your skills, making you a much stronger and more capable social work student who will be better placed to meet the needs of vulnerable service users. And second, to ensure that you are not expected to undertake those learning opportunities alone. Your practice educator is there to explore your strengths and areas for development and explore collaborative ways that harnesses your strengths and their expertise to maximise your learning.

■ PLACEMENT PERSPECTIVE 10.1 ■

NQSW reflection on learning in social work placement

Across my two placements I had lots of opportunities that have prepared me for my ASYE year. They developed my confidence hugely. I have developed my relationship skills with both adults and children with a wide range of complexities. I feel able to manage a busy workload even when unexpected things happen. I feel confident in a range of settings such as chairing meetings, leading on visits and carrying out meaningful direct work.

My placements provided the opportunity to develop my assessment skills, which has being crucial. A huge help was developing knowledge of available services in the community and really understanding interprofessional working. I was worried that I had very little relevant knowledge and that I would fail to appropriately identify risks. My practice educator was a huge source of support. I struggle to learn from reading. Instead my practice educator provided me with

(Continued)

assessment tools and practice scenarios where I was able to highlight the risks and identify risk management options, which really developed my confidence.

My supervisions were a huge help because they provided a safe space in which I could reflect. I was able to identify ways to enhance my practice and new models to use in practice. I developed my confidence in identifying theories I had used and was able to discuss my feelings and manage them successfully. We discussed working with service users with a wide range of problems, which has developed my emotional resilience which is essential in practice.

I also found that my team was very supportive. Just observing different social workers helped

as often different social workers would have a different approach. Some social workers were more risk averse than the others, and I observed case discussions in the team from which I gained confidence that you are not alone in making decisions as they are often complex.

My placements and practice educators really supported my development and confidence. My advice to any social work student starting placement is to take advantage of all the learning opportunities you can, even the ones that put you out of your comfort zone. Also, to ask any questions you have – sometimes they even help experienced workers expand their knowledge too.

Sophie Turnbull, NQSW

Initially, the book considered the processes that you will have experienced as a social work student preparing for and being on placement. This included the importance of knowing yourself and being open to reflection and exploration of your areas for development. The chapters went on to reflect on the relationships that you develop whilst on placement, including those with your practice educator and service users, both of which were considered critical to you maximising your practice learning opportunities. This also included consideration of the complexities of constructive feedback and ultimately concerns raised about your practice, with a view to enhancing your skills. The book then discussed the skills, knowledge and values you need to understand and sustain your working relationships, and went on to consider how these could be applied to the academic demands of the placement.

As you come to the end of your placement, you will have been asked to consider your learning from that placement, often summarised in an evidence folder, as discussed in Chapter 8, and/or an academic assignment, as discussed in Chapter 9. You may have been asked to reflect upon your learning needs as part of the process, or within final supervision with your practice educator.

Reflective Task 10.1

As you complete your final days on placement and look forward to your next period in university and further placement or your post-qualification career, what learning needs can you identify that you would like to continue to develop?

This should cover a holistic range of interventions skills, knowledge, value and diversity issues, reflective skills and professionalism. This should not be a final self-beating, but a reflective task that enables you to acknowledge that no matter how long you have been qualified, you will always have areas to develop. Indeed, Tham and Lynch (2014) undertook research which concluded that social work students rarely felt competent for qualified practice, but that their social work education had developed them and enabled them to understand the importance of reflective practice for their ongoing development. Similarly, McSweeney and Williams (2019) found that ASYE social workers were able to reflect on their placement as a critical foundation to develop both their practical and theoretical knowledge that underpins their practice, but offered advice to continue to build on this. Social work demands continuous professional development, so learning needs as you move forward should be a norm rather than a critique. Your practice educator should supply constructive future learning needs within your final report. As with all feedback, and as discussed in Chapter 7, take time to reflect on these issues as they will be the areas for you to build upon.

However, as you move into your next placement or first post-qualification post, I would urge to take the strengths that you have developed with you. Consider the transferable skills you have learnt in this placement. For example, whilst you might undertake a different assessment with a different service user group or service provision, your knowledge and experience of types of assessment (Smale et al., 1993) still apply. Your knowledge of motivational interviewing, both theoretically and in practice, will be highly beneficial and transferable in future settings. Your understanding of the oppression faced by adults who experience mental health and the communication skills developed in this placement will be invaluable for future roles, as mental health issues impact on many social work interventions. Take a little time to acknowledge your development over the placement period.

.... **Reflective Task 10.2** ....

Reflect back to your first week on placement. Imagine you are showing yourself around the placement, and tell yourself all the positive experiences you have had on that placement. Describe your learning from this placement.

I would like to end this book on a positive note: you have developed skills and knowledge over the period of your placement, so celebrate for a moment.

Good luck in your future social work career. Remember that your destiny is in your hands – you can be the social worker that you choose to be. If you believe that you can empower service users and challenge injustice, then you will be beginning to make positive changes in people's lives.

Paula

REFERENCES

Arendt, V. (2015) '5 ways to ace your social work interview', *The New Social Worker*, Winter: 8–9.

Arnstein, S. (1969) 'A ladder of citizen participation', *Journal of the American Planning Association*, 35 (4): 216–24.

Atwal, A. (2019) 'Reflective practice for interprofessional co-produced social work collaboration', in Mantell, A. and Scragg, T. (2019) *Reflective Practice in Social Work*. London: SAGE. pp. 172–87.

Bandura, A. (1977) *Social Learning Theory*. Englewood Cliffs, NJ: Prentice Hall.

Banks, S. (2016) 'Professional integrity: from conformity to commitment', in Hugman, R. and Carter, J. (eds) (2016) *Rethinking Values and Ethics in Social Work*. London: Palgrave. pp. 49–63.

Bassot, B. (2016) *The Reflective Journal*. London: Palgrave.

Beckett, C. and Horner, N. (2016) *Essential Theory for Social Workers*. London: SAGE.

Beckett, C., Maynard, A. and Jordan, P. (2017) *Values and Ethics in Social Work*. London: SAGE.

Beckett, S. (1983) *Worstward Ho*. London: John Calder.

Beesley, P., Watts, M. and Harrison, M. (2018) *Developing Your Communication Skills in Social Work*. London: SAGE.

Bell, J. (2018) 'Values and ethics', in Lishman, J., Yuill, C., Brannan, J. and Gibson, A. (eds) (2018) *Social Work: An Introduction*. London: SAGE. pp. 3–18.

Benner, K. and Curl, A. (2018) 'Exhausted, stressed, and disengaged: does employment create burnout for social work students?', *Journal of Social Work Education*, 54 (2): 300–9.

Blake, R. and Mouton, J. (1964) *The Managerial Grid*. Houston, TX: Gulf.

Boddy, J., O'Leary, P., Tsui, M., Pak, C. and Wang, D. (2018) 'Inspiring hope through social work practice', *International Social Work*, 61 (4): 587–99.

Bottomley, J., Cartney, P. and Pryjmachuk, S. (2018) *Studying for your Social Work Degree*. St Albans: Critical Publishing.

Bradley, G. (2008) 'The induction of newly appointed social workers: some implications for social work educators', *Social Work Education*, 27 (4): 349–65.

Brannan, J., Cromar, D., Gardner, S., Junner, M., Morrison, S. and Rae, W. (2018) 'The voice of service users and carers', in Lishman, J., Yuill, C., Brannan, J. and Gibson, A. (eds) (2018) *Social Work: An Introduction*. London: SAGE. pp. 251–64.

British Association of Social Workers (BASW) (2013) *Practice Educator Professional Standards for Social Work*. Available at www.basw.co.uk/resources/practice-educator-professional-standards-social-work?id=4784 (accessed 16 April 2019).

British Association of Social Workers (BASW) (2014) *Code of Ethics*. Available at www.basw.co.uk/about-basw/code-ethics (accessed 16 April 2019).

British Association of Social Workers (BASW) (2018) *Student PCF Level Descriptors for Pre-qualifying Levels and ASYE*. Available at www.basw.co.uk/resources/student-pcf-level-descriptors-pre-qualifying-levels-and-asye (accessed 16 April 2019).

Butler, G. (2019) 'Reflecting on emotion in social work', in Mantell, A. and Scragg, T. (2019) *Reflective Practice in Social Work*. London: SAGE. pp. 39–62.

Burg, M., Schwartz, J., Kronish, I., Diaz, K., Alcantara, C., Duer-Hefele, J. and Davidson, K. (2017) 'Does stress result in you exercising less? Or does exercising result in you being less stressed? Or is it both? Testing the bi-directional stress-exercise association at the group and person (N of 1) Level', *Annals of Behavioral Medicine*, 51 (6): 799–809.

Cabiati, E. and Folgheraiter, F. (2019) 'Let's try to change ourselves first: an action-research on experiential learning with social work students' *Social Work Education*, 38 (4).

Carter, J. and Hugman, R. (2016) 'Social work ethics and values in turbulent times', in Hugman, R. and Carter, J. (eds) (2016) *Rethinking Values and Ethics in Social Work*. London: Palgrave. pp. 1–15.

Cartwright, L. (2017) 'Supporting students to use social media and comply with professional standards', *Social Work Education*, 36 (8): 880–92.

Casement, P. (1985) *On Learning from the Patient*. London: Tavistock.

Collen, K. (2019) 'Education for a sustainable future? Students' experiences of workshops on ethical dilemmas', *Social Work Education*, 38 (1): 119–28.

Collingwood, P. (2005) 'Integrating theory and practice: the three-stage theory framework', *Journal of Practice Teaching*, 6 (1): 6–23.

Cooper, B. (2010) 'Getting the best from social work degree placements', *Community Care*, 20 (9).

Croisdale-Appleby, D. (2014) *Re-visioning Social Work Education: An Independent Review*. London: Department of Health and Social Care.

Davys, A. and Beddoe, L. (2010) *A Guide for the Helping Professions*. London: Jessica Kingsley.

Department for Education (DfE) (2018) *Post-qualifying Standard: Knowledge and Skills Statement for Child and Family Practitioners*. London: HMSO.

Department of Health (DoH) (2015) *Knowledge and Skills Statement for Social Workers in Adult Services*. London: HMSO.

Doel, M. (2010) *Social Work Placements: A Traveller's Guide*. Oxford: Routledge.

Doel, M. (2018) 'Preface', in Taplin, S. (ed.) (2018) *Innovations in Practice Learning*. St Albans: Critical Publishing. pp. xi–xv.

Driscoll, J. (2007) *Practising Clinical Supervision: A Reflective Approach for Healthcare Professionals*. Edinburgh: Elsevier.

Dunk-West, P. (2018) *Practising Social Work Sociologically: A Theoretical approach for New Times*. London: Palgrave.

Edmondson, D. (2014) *Social Work Practice Learning: A Student Guide*. London: SAGE.

Egan, R. Maidment, J. and Connolly, M. (2017) 'Trust, power and safety in the social work supervisory relationship: results from Australian research', *Journal of Social Work Practice*, 31 (3): 307–21.

Feiler, A. and Powell, D. (2016) 'Behavioural expression of job interview anxiety', *Journal of Business and Psychology*, 31 (1): 155–71.

Fenge, L., Howe, K., Hughes, M. and Thomas, G. (2014) *The Social Work Portfolio: A Student's Guide to Evidencing your Practice*. Maidenhead: Open University Press.

Ferguson, H. (2018) 'How social workers reflect in action and when and why they don't: the possibilities and limits to reflective practice in social work', *Social Work Education*, 37 (4): 415–27.

Finch, J. (2017) *Supporting Struggling Students on Placement*. Bristol: Policy Press.

Finch, J. and Taylor, I. (2013) 'The emotional experience of assessing a struggling or failing social work student in practice learning settings', *Special Edition – Field Education, Social Work Education*, 32 (2): 244–58.

Flanagan, N. and Wilson, E. (2018) 'What makes a good placement? Findings of a social work student-to-student research study', *Social Work Education*, 37 (5): 565–80.

Fleming, N. and Mills, C. (1992) 'Not another inventory, rather a catalyst for reflection', *To Improve the Academy*, 11: 137–55.

Fook, J. (2014) *Social Work: A Critical Approach to Practice*. London: SAGE.

Fook, J. and Gardner, F. (2007) *Practising Critical Reflection: A Resource Handbook*. Maidenhead: Open University Press.

Foucault, M. (1979) *Discipline and Punish*. Harmondsworth: Penguin.

Frith, L. and Martin, R. (2015) *Professional Writing Skills for Social Workers*. Maidenhead: Open University Press.

Gardner, F. (2014) *Being Critically Reflective*. London: Palgrave.

Gibbs, G. (1988) *Learning by Doing: A Guide to Teaching and Learning Methods*. Oxford: Further Education Unit, Oxford Polytechnic.

Gill, J. and Medd, W. (2015) *Get Sorted: How to Make the Most of Your Student Experience*. London: Palgrave.

Green, P. and Crisp, B. (2007) 'Critical incident analyses: a practice learning tool for students and practioners', *Social Work in Action*, 19 (1): 1.

Greenaway, R. (2014) *Doing Reviewing*. Available at http://reviewing.co.uk/articles/reviewing_outdoorsx3.htm (accessed 16 April 2019).

Greer, J. (2016) *Resilience and Personal Effectiveness for Social Workers*. London: SAGE.

Greetham, B. (2018) *How to Write Better Essays*. London: Palgrave.

Hart, A. (2018) 'Reflective practice', in Lishman, J., Yuill, C., Brannan, J. and Gibson, A. (eds) (2018) *Social Work: An Introduction*. London: SAGE. pp. 153–70.

Health and Care Professions Council (HCPC) (2016) *Standards on Conduct Performance and Ethics*. London: HCPC.

Health and Care Professions Council (HCPC) (2017a) *Guidance on Conduct and Ethics for Students*. London: HCPC.

Health and Care Professions Council (HCPC) (2017b) *Standards on Proficiency: Social Workers in England*. London: HCPC.

Healy, K. (2018) *The Skilled Communicator in Social Work: The Art and Science of Communication in Practice*. London: Palgrave.

Heffer, T. and Willoughby, T. (2017) 'A count of coping strategies: a longitudinal study investigating an alternative method to understanding coping and adjustment', *PLoS ONE*, 12 (10).

Heron, G., McGoldrick, R. and Wilson, R. (2015) 'Exploring the influence of feedback on student social workers' understanding of childcare and protection', *British Journal of Social Work*, 45 (8): 2317–34.

Higgins, M. (2019) 'Getting started', in Mantell, A. and Scragg, T. (2019) *Reflective Practice in Social Work*. London: SAGE. pp. 19–38.

Hill, D., Agu, L. and Mercer, D. (2019) *Exploring and Locating Social Work*. London: Red Globe.

Honey, P. and Mumford, A. (1986) *A Manual of Learning Styles*. Maidenhead: Peter Honey Publications.

Howe, D. (2008) *The Emotionally Intelligent Social Worker*. London: Palgrave.

Howe, D. (2013) *Empathy: What it is and Why it Matters*. London: Palgrave.

Hughes, M. (2017) 'What difference does it make? Findings of an impact study of service user and carer involvement on social work students' subsequent practice', *Social Work Education*, 36 (2): 203–16.

Hugman, R. and Carter, J. (eds) (2016) *Rethinking Values and Ethics in Social Work*. London: Palgrave.

Hunt, R. and Mathews, I. (2018) 'Supporting students with dyslexia on placement: theory into practice', in Taplin, S. (ed.) *Innovations in Practice Learning*. St Albans: Critical Publishing. pp. 121–36.

Illeris, K. (2014) *Transformative Learning and Identity*. Abingdon: Routledge.

Ingram, R. (2015) *Understanding Emotions in Social Work*. Maidenhead: Open University Press.

Ingram, R., Fenton, J., Hodson, A. and Jindal-Snape, D. (2014) *Reflective Social Work Practice*. London: Palgrave.

Jasper, M. (2003) *Beginning Reflective Practice*. Cheltenham: Nelson Thornes.

Jones, S. (2015) *Social Work Practice Placements*. London: SAGE.

Kay, E. and Curington, A. (2018) 'Preparing masters' students for social work practice: the perspective of field instructors', *Social Work Education*, 37 (8): 968–76.

Knott, C. (2013) 'Reflective practice revisited', in Knott, C. and Scragg, T. (2013) *Reflective Practice in Social Work*. London: SAGE. pp. 9–21.

Knott, C. and Scragg, T. (2013) *Reflective Practice in Social Work*. London: SAGE.

Knowles, M. (1973) *The Adult Learner: A Neglected Species*. Houston, TX: Gulf.

Kolb, D. A. (1984) *Experiential Learning: Experience as the Source of Learning and Development*, Vol. 1. Englewood Cliffs, NJ: Prentice-Hall.

Kuusisaari, H. (2014) 'Teachers at the zone of proximal development: collaboration promoting or hindering the development process', *Teaching and Teacher Education*, 43: 46–57.

Kwan, C. and Reupert, A. (2019) 'The relevance of social workers' personal experiences to their practices', *The British Journal of Social Work*, 49 (1): 256–71.

Laird, S. and Tedam, P. (2019) *Cultural Diversity in Child Protection*. Red Globe Press: London

Laming, Lord H. (2003) *The Victoria Climbié Inquiry: Report of an Inquiry by Lord Laming*. London: HMSO.

Lishman, J., Yuill, C., Brannan, J. and Gibson, A. (eds) (2018) *Social Work: An Introduction*. London: SAGE.

Lomax, R. and Jones, K. (2014) *Surviving your Social Work Placement*. London: Palgrave Macmillan.

Luft, J. and Ingham, H. (1955) 'The Johari Window: a graphic model of interpersonal awareness', in *Proceedings of the Western Training Laboratory in Group Development*, Los Angeles, University of California.

Maclean, S. and Harrison, R. (2015) *A Straightforward Guide to Theory for Social Work Students*. Lichfield: Kirwin Maclean Associates.

Maclean, S., Finch, J. and Tedam, T. (2018) *SHARE*. Lichfield: Kirwin Maclean.

Mantell, A. (2019) 'The importance of the perspective of carer and service users', in Mantell, A. and Scragg, T. (2019) *Reflective Practice in Social Work*. London: SAGE. pp. 83–106.

Mantell, A. and Scragg, T (2019) *Reflective Practice in Social Work*. London: SAGE.

Matthews, I., Simpson, D. and Crawford, K. (2014) *Your Social Work Practice Placement: From Start to Finish*. London: SAGE.

McSweeney, F. and Williams, D. (2019) 'Social care graduates' judgements of their readiness and preparedness for practice', *Social Work Education*, 38 (3).

Miehls, D., Everett, J., Segal, C. and du Bois, C. (2013) 'MSW students' views of supervision: factors contributing to satisfactory field experiences', *The Clinical Supervisor*, 32 (1): 128–46.

Miller, W. and Rollnick, S. (1991) *Motivational Interviewing: Preparing People to Change Addictive Behaviour*. New York: Guilford Press.

Munro, E. (2017) *The Munro Review of Child Protection: Final Report: A Child-Centred System*. London: Department for Education.

Musson, P. (2011) *Effective Writing Skills for Social Work Students*. London: SAGE.

Nicholas, W. and Kerr, J. (2015) *Practice Educating Social Work Students: Supporting Qualifying Students on their Placement*. Maidenhead: Open University Press.

Oliver, C., Jones, E., Rayner, A., Penner, J. and Jamieson, A. (2017) 'Teaching social work students to speak up', *Social Work Education*, 36 (6): 702–14.

Palma-Garcia, M., Jacinto, L. and Hombrados, I. (2018) 'Reciprocal relationship between resilience and professional skills: a longitudinal study with social work students', *Journal of Social Work Education*, 54 (3): 532–42.

Papouli, E. (2014) 'The development of professional social work values and ethics in the workplace: a critical incident analysis from the students' perspective'. PhD dissertation, University of Sussex.

Papouli, E. (2016) 'Using the critical incident technique (CIT) to explore how students develop their understanding of social work values and ethics in the workplace during their final placement', *Journal of Social Work Values & Ethics*, 13 (2): 56–72.

Pearl, R., Williams, H., Williams, L., Brown, K., Brown, B., Hollington, L., Gruffydd, M., Jones, R., Yorke, S. and Statham, G. (2018) 'Service user and carer feedback: simply pass/fail or a genuine learning tool?', *Social Work Education*, 37 (5): 553–64.

Prochaska, J. and DiClemente, C. (1983) 'Stages and processes of self-change in smoking: toward an integrative model of change', *Journal of Consulting and Clinical Psychology*, 5: 390–95.

Race, P. (2007) *The Lecturer's Toolkit: A Practical Guide to Assessment, Learning and Teaching*. Abingdon: Routledge.

Rankine, M, Beddoe, L, O'Brien, M, and Fouché, C (2018) 'What's your agenda? Reflective supervision in community-based child welfare services', *European Journal of Social Work*, 21(3): 428–40.

Rook, S. (2013) *The Graduate Career Guidebook: Advice for Students and Graduates on Careers Options, Jobs, Volunteering, Applications, Interviews and Self-employment*. London: Palgrave.

Roulston, A., Cleak, H. and Vreugdenhil, A. (2018) 'Promoting readiness to practice: which learning activities promote competence and professional identity for student social workers during practice learning?', *Journal of Social Work Education*, 54 (2): 364–78.

Sadd, J. (2011) '"We are more than our story": Service user and carer participation in social work education', SCIE Report 42. London: Social Care Institute for Excellence.

Sadler, D. (2010) 'Beyond feedback: developing student capability in complex appraisal', *Assessment and Evaluation in Higher Education*, 35: 535–50.

Saltiel, D. (2017) 'Supervision: a contested space for learning and decision making', *Qualitative Social Work*, 16 (4): 533–49.

Schmidt, B., Warns, L., Hellmer, M., Ulrich, N. and Hewig, J. (2018) 'What makes us feel good or bad mood: induction and individual differences in a job interview setting', *Journal of Individual Differences*, 39 (3): 142–50.

Schon, D. (1983) *The Reflective Practitioner*. London: Maurice Temple Smith.

Scragg, T. (2019) 'Reflective practice on placement', in Mantell, A. and Scragg, T. (2019) *Reflective Practice in Social Work*. London: SAGE. pp. 139–54.

Sennett, R. (2008) *The Craftsman*. London: Allen Lane.

Sicora, A. (2019) 'Reflective practice and learning from mistakes in social work student placement', *Social Work Education*, 38 (1): 63–74.

Smale, B. and Fowlie, J. (2015) *How to Succeed at University*. London: SAGE.

Smale, G., Tuson, G., Biehal, N. and Marsh, P. (1993) *Empowerment, Assessment, Care Management and the Skilled Worker*. London: HMSO.

Speers, J. and Lathlean, J. (2015) 'Service user involvement in giving mental health students feedback on placement: a participatory action research study', *Nursing Education Today*, 35 (9): 84–9.

Stogdon, C. and Kiteley, R. (2010) *Study Skills for Social Workers*. London: SAGE.

Stone, C. (2018) 'Transparency of assessment in practice education: the TAPE model', *Social Work Education*, 37 (8): 977–94.

Sutton, C. (1994) *Social Work, Community Work and Psychology*. Leicester: BPS Books.

Taplin, S. (ed.) (2018) *Innovations in Practice Learning*. St Albans: Critical Publishing.

Tedam, P. (2012) 'The MANDELA model of practice learning: an old present in new wrapping?', *Journal of Practice Teaching and Learning*, 11 (2): 60–76.

Tedam, P. (2015) 'Enhancing the practice learning experiences of BME students: strategies for practice education', *Journal of Practice Teaching and Learning*, 13 (2–3): 130–45.

Tham, P. and Lynch, D. (2014) 'Prepared for practice? Graduating social work students' reflections on their education, competence and skills', *Social Work Education*, 33 (6): 704–17.

Thompson, N. (1992) *Anti-Discriminatory Practice*. London: Palgrave.

Thompson, N. (2012) *Anti-Discriminatory Practice* (3rd edn). London: Palgrave.

Thompson, N. (2016) *The Professional Social Worker*. London: Palgrave.

Tripp, D. (1993) *Critical Incidents in Teaching: Developing Professional Judgement*. London: Routledge.

Vygotsky, L. (1978) *Mind and Society: The Development of Higher Psychological Processes*. Cambridge, MA: Harvard University Press.

Walid, E., Hamed, A. and Oskrochi, R. (2014) 'Food and mental health: relationship between food and perceived stress and depressive symptoms among university students in the United Kingdom', *Central European Journal of Public Health*, 22 (2): 90–97.

Weaver, H. (1999) 'Culture and professional education the experiences of native American social workers', *Journal of Social Work Education*, 36 (3): 217–25.

Westwood, J. (2019) *Social Media in Social Work Practice*. London: SAGE.

Whitaker, L. and Reimer, E. (2017) 'Students' conceptualisations of critical reflection', *Social Work Education*, 36 (8): 946–58.

INDEX